POEMS THAT MAKE GROWN MEN CRY

100 Men on the Words
that Move Them

Edited by

ANTHONY and BEN HOLDEN

SIMON
SCHUST

<blockquote>London · New York · Sydney

A CBS CON</blockquote>

First published in Great Britain by Simon & Schuster UK Ltd, 2014
This paperback edition published by Simon & Schuster UK Ltd, 2015
A CBS COMPANY

Copyright © 2014 by Anthony Holden and Ben Holden

This book is copyright under the Berne Convention.
No reproduction without permission.
All rights reserved.

The right of Anthony Holden and Ben Holden to be identified as the
authors of this work has been asserted by them in accordance with sections
77 and 78 of the Copyright, Designs and Patents Act, 1988.

WEST DUNBARTONSHIRE LIBRARIES	
C 03 0262497	
Askews & Holts	21-Apr-2016
808.81	£9.99
DA	

ISBN: 978-1-47113-490-6
ebook ISBN: 978-1-47113-491-3

The author and publishers have made all reasonable efforts
to contact copyright-holders for permission, and apologise
for any omissions or errors in the form of credits given.
Corrections may be made to future printings.

Interior design by Ruth Lee-Mui

Printed and bound by CPI Group (UK) Ltd, Croydon, CR0 4YY

Contents

Contents

Preface

ANTHONY HOLDEN

Late one afternoon in the mid-1990s a close friend of long standing called to tell me of a sudden domestic crisis. My wife and I went straight round to join him for the evening, during which he began to quote a Thomas Hardy poem, 'The Darkling Thrush'. Upon reaching what might be called the punch line – 'Some blessed Hope, whereof he knew / And I was unaware' – our friend choked up, unable to get the words out. This was understandable: he was still upset by the day's events. We ourselves were much moved.

That weekend we happened to be visiting the scholar and critic Frank Kermode. Frank knew the friend involved, and was also touched by his Hardy moment. 'Is there any poem *you* can't recite without choking up?' I asked him. Never an emotionally demonstrative man, Frank said immediately: 'Go and get the Larkin.'

In front of his half-dozen guests he then began to read aloud 'Unfinished Poem', about death treading its remorseless way up the stairs, only to turn out to be a pretty young girl with bare feet, moving the stunned narrator to exclaim: 'What summer have you broken from?' It was this startling last line that rendered Frank speechless; with a forlorn waft of the hand, he held the book out for someone else to finish the poem.

Also there that day was another professor of English, Tony

Tanner, so it was not surprising that this topic of conversation lasted all afternoon, ranging far and wide, not just over other candidates for this distinct brand of poetic immortality but the power of poetry over prose to move, the difference between true sentiment and mere mawkishness, and, of course, the pros and cons of men weeping, whether in private or in public.

For the next few weeks I asked every male literary friend I saw to name a poem he couldn't read or recite without breaking up. It was amazing how many immediately said yes, this one, and embarked on its first few lines. With Frank's encouragement, I began to contemplate an anthology called *Poems that Make Strong Men Cry*.

Then I remembered I had another book to finish, and set the project aside. But it remained a topic of paradoxically happy conversation between Frank and myself until his death in the summer of 2010, at the age of ninety. I duly steeled myself to reading 'Unfinished Poem' at his funeral service and managed it – just – without choking up.

In 2007, reviewing A. E. Housman's letters for the *London Review of Books*, Kermode had discussed the controversy caused in Cambridge in 1933 by a Housman lecture entitled 'On the Name and Nature of Poetry'. After recalling the brouhaha provoked at the time by Housman's emphasis on the emotional power of poetry, with F. R. Leavis saying it would 'take years to remedy the damage the lecture must have inflicted on his students', Frank continued – with, he told me, our recurrently lachrymose conversation very much in mind:

> What everybody remembers best are the passages about the emotional aspects of poetry. Housman included a number of surprisingly personal comments on this topic. Milton's 'Nymphs and shepherds, dance no more', he said, can 'draw tears . . . to the eyes of more readers than one.' And tears are only one

symptom. A line of poetry can make his beard bristle as he shaves, or cause a shiver down his spine, or 'a constriction of the throat' as well as 'a precipitation of water to the eyes'. For so reticent a man it was a surprising performance. It possibly upset his health, and he came to regard the date of the lecture, May 1933, as an ominous moment in his life.

Housman and Hardy have emerged as two of the most tear-provoking poets in this collection – to which I was urged to return, in the wake of Frank's death, by my son Ben (if with a somewhat less *macho* title). With three entries each, they are equalled by Philip Larkin and bested only by W. H. Auden, with five. So four of us supposedly buttoned-up Brits top the charts of almost one hundred poems from eighteen countries, a dozen of them written by women, chosen by men of more than twenty nationalities ranging in age from early twenties to late eighties. Five pairs of contributors happen to have chosen the same poem, for intriguingly different reasons.

Larkin himself could have proved a prototype contributor. 'Wordsworth was nearly the price of me once,' he told the *Observer* in 1979. 'I was driving down the M1 on a Saturday morning: they had this poetry slot on the radio . . . and someone suddenly started reading the Immortality Ode, and I couldn't see for tears. And when you're driving down the middle lane at seventy miles an hour . . .'

Early in our task, we were encouraged by a note from Professor John Carey, with whom I discussed our work-in-progress over a dinner at Merton College, Oxford, where Ben and I both studied English thirty years apart: 'It will bring some good poems to public notice, and it will stimulate debate about the emotional power of art and how it affects different people.' Thanks to our partnership with Amnesty International, we can add such cross-border issues as freedom of speech and thought, as in the contribution from one of the leaders of the 1989 human rights protests in Beijing's Tiananmen Square.

After deciding to arrange the poems in chronological order, we calculated that some 75 per cent of them were written in the twentieth century – inevitable, perhaps, so early in the twenty-first. The most common themes, apart from intimations of mortality, range from pain and loss via social and political ideals to the beauty and variety of Nature – as well as love, in all its many guises. Three of our contributors have suffered the ultimate pain of losing a child; others are moved to tears by the sheer beauty of the way a poet captures, in Alexander Pope's famous phrase, 'what oft was thought, but ne'er so well express'd'. The same might be said of our contributors' candid explanations of their choices, many of which rival the poems themselves in stirring the reader's emotions.

Some of those who declined to take part did so for almost poetic reasons. Wrote the pianist Alfred Brendel: 'I easily shed tears when I listen to music, experience a Shakespeare play, or encounter a great performance. Literature doesn't have the same effect on me, so it seems. I cannot tell you why, as reading has been an important part of my life.' Said the actor-magician Ricky Jay: 'Right now, I find it hard to think of a poem that *doesn't* make me cry. I'm the kinda guy that weeps at reruns of *Happy Days*.' And the playwright Patrick Marber: 'You bet I've got one, but I'm not going to share it with anyone else!'

A sudden shock of emotion naturally overcomes different people in different ways. Vladimir Nabokov wrote that the proper reader responds to a poem not with his brain or his heart, but with his back, waiting for 'the telltale tingle between the shoulder-blades'. To our contributors, a moist eye seems the natural if involuntary response to a particular phrase or line, thought or image; the vast majority are public figures not prone to tears, as is supposedly the manly way, but here prepared to admit to caving in when ambushed by great art.

→ ←

The youngest of my three sons, now himself a father, Ben, is a grown man to whom tears do not come readily; I myself, as he has enjoyed telling all enquirers, am prone to weep all too easily, at prose as much as poetry, movies as much as music. We've had a great deal of fun, and not a few vigorous disagreements, while compiling this anthology together.

It was only after intense negotiation, for instance, that we agreed to stretch most definitions of poetry by including an extract from a verse play, and another from a 'prose-poem' of a novel, then another, while drawing the line at song lyrics – some of which are fine poetry, for sure, but (in my view) indistinguishable in their power to move from the music to which they are set. We agreed to admit one traditional lullaby; but this policy otherwise cost us, alas, a distinguished writer intent on a touching French *chanson*, and an astronaut who wanted the lyric of a song from a Broadway musical.

On which note, I am pleased to hand over to Ben for an expert explanation of the physical mechanics of tears, especially male tears, and to distil perfectly on both our behalves the purpose, as we see it, of this book.

BEN HOLDEN

Cecil Day-Lewis once said that he did not write poetry to be understood, but to understand. This quest, to understand, takes many routes but is common to us all. Tears also unite us as humans: we are the only species that cries. Charles Darwin himself was at a loss to explain this uniquely human trait, describing it as that 'special expression of man's'.

One scientific explanation is that the act of crying is evolution's mechanism for draining excess chemicals released into the blood when we experience extreme stress or high emotion: the chin's mentalis muscle wobbles; a lump rises in our throat, as the autonomic nervous system expands the glottis to aid our oxygen intake; the lachrymal glands flood the fornix conjunctiva of the upper eyelid; and, as teardrops break their ducts and run down our cheeks, our blood is cleansed of the secreted prolactin and adrenocorticotropic hormones.

Put another way: we have 'a good cry' and feel better.

An alternative theory is that crying is an advancement of a mammalian distress signal. After all, tears provide a clear and immediate cry for help that is tricky to fake. And just as it is tough to counterfeit, crying can also be catching, like yawning. One person's tears often set off another's.

In these ways, weeping betrays not only vulnerability but also an openness that is contagious. Yet so often we try to hide our tears when caught out or in public, as if it is embarrassing to be around such raw tenderness. This is perhaps especially true for those of us who are men.

Despite the male tear duct being larger than the female, studies have consistently shown that from around the age of ten a divergence occurs and thereafter boys cry far less than girls. Whether that is down to cultural or biological reasons (or, as is likely the case, both), the sad truth is that the male of our species has not always been allowed to cry. Tears may have been venerated in European cultures during the nineteenth century as a sign of high moral character but, these days, they are all too hastily wiped away.

We want to put paid to that with this anthology. We hope that readers may set each other off as they read these verses aloud to one another. Let's celebrate high emotion! Together let's express our shared humanity, whatever your gender, background or circumstances. However grievous at times, let these pages console you, if upset; lift you, if down; I defy you not to be inspired by them.

To borrow from Samuel Beckett, our contributors' 'words are their tears'. Some of their introductions are profoundly moving and many describe devastating ordeals. These woes are framed in personal contexts but will be familiar to many readers. During its compilation, contributor Billy Collins jokingly asked how any of us will make it through the book without succumbing to a complete emotional breakdown. Yet our intent with this collection is to celebrate our shared compassion and common humanity, all in keeping with the creed of our partners at Amnesty International.

We hope as you read these pages that your own corneas may at times flood. Crying expresses our very inability to articulate emotion, after all, and so what could be more human, honest, or pure than tears?

Perhaps the only response is that other 'special expression' of ours: poetry.

POEMS
THAT MAKE
GROWN MEN
CRY

Elegy

CHIDIOCK TICHBORNE (1563–86)

→ ←

DAVID McVICAR

Tichborne died at around age twenty-three in 1586, a conspirator in the infamous Babington Plot to assassinate Elizabeth I and rescue Mary Stuart from captivity. The poem was written as part of a letter to his wife, Agnes, days before the hideous sentence for traitors was carried out, and he was executed. It's a beautifully constructed elegy, as would be expected from an educated gentleman of the period. The use of paradox to describe his mental state reaches out beyond the personal and touches upon the universal human condition.

These are technical points. It moves and terrifies me so much because the poet is here composing his own elegy. The immediacy of these lines, as their author reflects upon the waste of his brief life and faces a death of indescribable agony, touches me in a way that's hard to put into words. The certain knowledge of and the struggle to accept death seems to me a primary motor of the artistic impulse; why we create art and why we turn to art and how art helps us to express whatever is valid or has meaning in our short span of existence.

Elegy

My prime of youth is but a frost of cares,
My feast of joy is but a dish of pain,
My crop of corn is but a field of tares,
And all my good is but vain hope of gain;
The day is past, and yet I saw no sun,
And now I live, and now my life is done.

My tale was heard and yet it was not told,
My fruit is fallen, and yet my leaves are green,
My youth is spent and yet I am not old,
I saw the world and yet I was not seen;
My thread is cut and yet it is not spun,
And now I live, and now my life is done.

I sought my death and found it in my womb,
I looked for life and saw it was a shade,
I trod the earth and knew it was my tomb,
And now I die, and now I was but made;
My glass is full, and now my glass is run,
And now I live, and now my life is done.

(1586)

→ ←

Productions by the Scottish opera director Sir David McVicar (b. 1966) have been seen at the Royal Opera House, Covent Garden, the Metropolitan Opera, Glyndebourne, Chicago Lyric Opera, English National Opera, Scottish Opera, the Mariinsky Theatre, St Petersburg, and at many other theatres around the world.

Sonnet XXX

WILLIAM SHAKESPEARE (1564–1616)

→ ←

MELVYN BRAGG

I have never been able to read this sonnet to the end without stumbling and then stopping. It is the final couplet that finishes me off and yet it says the opposite of what the poem has made me feel so acutely.

All great poems are about each one of us. This speaks as directly to me over the centuries as any evening's call from a close friend. What is described is a condition we all find ourselves in and increasingly so as we age.

For me it paints a picture of my thoughts and feelings when I think of my first wife, who took her life more than forty years ago. I feel as responsible, as guilty, and as ashamed now as I was then. The first twelve lines bind the past to the present so accurately and poignantly that you see no division between them, and that, for me, is the great power of the piece.

In the poem Shakespeare moves from considerations of time, to friends, to love, to sights, and the resurrection of ancient 'woes'. All these magnetised my past and present feelings about Lise. And somehow his optimistic last two lines, which redeem the rest and even rebut it, are those I can never meet without tears. Perhaps because his 'dear friend' is living and mine is not.

Sonnet XXX

When to the sessions of sweet silent thought
I summon up remembrance of things past,
I sigh the lack of many a thing I sought,
And with old woes new wail my dear time's waste:
Then can I drown an eye, unused to flow,
For precious friends hid in death's dateless night,
And weep afresh love's long since cancelled woe,
And moan the expense of many a vanished sight:
Then can I grieve at grievances foregone,
And heavily from woe to woe tell o'er
The sad account of fore-bemoanéd moan,
Which I new pay as if not paid before.
But if the while I think on thee, dear friend,
All losses are restored and sorrows end.

(1609)

→ ←

The writer and broadcaster Melvyn Bragg (b. 1939) has published more than twenty novels, most recently *Grace and Mary* (2013), and fourteen works of nonfiction, including *The Adventure of English* (2003). He has also written two books for children and four screenplays, including *The Music Lovers* (1970) and *Jesus Christ Superstar* (1973). For several decades he has presented TV's *The South Bank Show* and BBC Radio's *In Our Time*. He was created a life peer in 1998.

On My First Son

BEN JONSON (1572–1637)

➤ ←

JOHN CAREY

I have, thank God, never lost a child. But every parent has a lurking dread that it may happen, and an inbuilt sympathy with those to whom it has. Over and above these obvious triggers of grief in Jonson's poem, though, it is the tone that makes it, for me, impossible – or anyway, unsafe – to try to read aloud.

I know, from experiment, that I cannot be sure to get any further than the last two words of the second line – 'loved boy'. They sound so natural, so like a loving afterthought, as if he has turned to the child and addressed him in an altered, gentler voice, as you might do after making some more public announcement – just to reassure him, in case he is afraid or bewildered. I think that, once that point is past, I could manage to read the rest. Jonson blaming himself, and consoling himself by thinking of the tribulations his child will not now have to suffer, reaches a kind of precarious equipoise, and by the end he's looking to the future. It's that 'loved boy' that's the killer.

On My First Son

Farewell, thou child of my right hand, and joy;
My sin was too much hope of thee, loved boy.
Seven years thou wert lent to me, and I thee pay,
Exacted by thy fate, on the just day.
O, could I lose all father now! For why
Will man lament the state he should envy?
To have so soon 'scap'd world's and flesh's rage,
And, if no other misery, yet age?
Rest in soft peace, and, asked, say, 'Here doth lie
Ben Jonson his best piece of poetry.'
For whose sake henceforth all his vows be such
As what he loves may never like too much.

(1616)

→ ←

John Carey (b. 1934) is emeritus Merton Professor of English Litera-
ture at the University of Oxford, twice chairman of the Man Booker
Prize judges, and a frequent broadcaster. Among his many published
works are studies of Milton, Dickens, Thackeray, Donne, and Golding,
a polemic entitled *What Good Are the Arts?* (2005), and his memoir,
The Unexpected Professor (2014).

Amor constante más allá de la muerte

FRANCISCO DE QUEVEDO (1580-1645)

➔ ◆

ARIEL DORFMAN

It is the last line that does it; the tears come from beyond me, and perhaps from beyond death. The eyes that shed those tears will become dust, the eyes that have seen over and over the love of my life, Angélica, the woman who helped me survive exile and tribulations and peopled my world with hope – those eyes will have been closed by the final shadow. And yet the *polvo*, the dust, is *enamorado*, is in love.

Except that there are no words in English that can offer us the equivalent of *enamorado* or *enamoramiento*, so much so that I have had a correspondence with my friend, the extraordinary Spanish author Javier Marías, about the right translation into English for his equally extraordinary novel, entitled *Los Enamoramientos*, and we reached the conclusion that there was no perfect fit for such a word, not in English, not in any language.

Quevedo knew this many centuries ago and finished his poem with that word, which tells us that we are filled with love, we fall into love as if into an abyss, we ascend to its invitation to *enamorar*, a verb that enhances what both lovers must do, make someone love me, find myself overflowing with love.

That last verse never fails to make me cry. The laws of the universe discovered by physics assure humanity that we are composed of atoms and that protons and neutrons and electrons will scatter and rejoin, that everything is connected, that when we drink a glass of water or shed a tear, some slight marrow of Shakespeare or Brecht or Rumi is submerged in the depths of the liquid coupling of hydrogen and oxygen: the cosmos as a giant blender, making our every cell ultimately immortal. I am not religious and do not believe, as Quevedo did, that the soul will subsist, that God will greet us once our body has finished its course of skin and bone and flesh. But this I do believe: my wife and I have sworn to mix our ashes, to be dust together for eternity. *Polvo seremos, mas polvo enamorado*. Angélica and I will be dust but dust in love. How can I not cry with joy for myself, for her, for all of us on this earth that will itself turn to dust, ashes to ashes, yes, but ashes in love.

JAVIER MARÍAS

As we grow older, perhaps what saddens us most about the prospect of death – and, oddly enough, what strikes us as most melancholy and un-bearable too – is not that we will cease to live and have no more future, that is, no more knowledge, curiosity, or laughter, but the certainty that all our memories, our past, will disappear along with us, that everything we have experienced, seen, heard, thought, and felt will no longer 'float' in the world – to use a deliberately imprecise verb.

Maybe that is what is so moving about any attempt to rebel against this future disappearance. Not, I repeat, the disappearance of our own selves, but of all that we preserve within us and that depends for its existence entirely upon our consciousness.

Quevedo's sonnet is one of the most successful of rebellions. It matters little that, as Borges pointed out, its extraordinary last lines are perhaps 'a re-creation, or an exaltation' of a line by Propertius (*Elegies*, Book I, 19). Quevedo's last two lines – the lines that bring a lump to the throat – are infinitely superior. As are the first two lines, which throw down the challenge: even though death may close my eyes and sweep me off on the blank white day – '*el blanco día*', that is, '*el día en blanco*', a marvelous way of describing the day on which nothing will be written and on which nothing will happen – even though my veins and my marrow and my whole body will be turned to ash, it will be ash that is still filled with meaning, and even though they will be dust, even though they will be nothing, they will be a nothing that still loves. Yes, this poem is one of the most sublime rebellions in the history of literature. And we, the living, continue to read it, and that, at least, is something.

Amor constante más allá de la muerte
Cerrar podrá mis ojos la postrera
Sombra que me llevare el blanco día,
Y podrá desatar esta alma mía
Hora a su afán ansioso lisonjera;

Mas no, de esotra parte, en la ribera,
Dejará la memoria, en donde ardía:
Nadar sabe mi llama el agua fría,
Y perder el respeto a ley severa.

Alma a quien todo un dios prisión ha sido,
Venas que humor a tanto fuego han dado,
Médulas que han gloriosamente ardido:

Su cuerpo dejará, no su cuidado;
Serán ceniza, mas tendrá sentido;
Polvo serán, mas polvo enamorado.

(PUBLISHED 1648)

Love Constant Beyond Death

Though my eyes be closed by the final
Shadow that sweeps me off on the blank white day
And thus my soul be rendered up
By fawning time to hastening death;

Yet memory will not abandon love
On the shore where first it burned:
My flame can swim through coldest water
And will not bend to laws severe.

Soul that was prison to a god,
Veins that fueled such fire,
Marrow that gloriously burned –

The body they will leave, though not its cares;
Ash they will be, but filled with meaning;
Dust they will be, but dust in love.

TRANSLATION BY MARGARET JULL COSTA

➔ ←

A Chilean-American citizen born in Argentina, the novelist and play-
wright Ariel Dorfman (b. 1942) has written many works in English
and Spanish, published in over fifty languages. His plays have been
performed in more than one hundred countries, including *Death and
the Maiden* (filmed in 1994 by Roman Polanski), *Purgatorio*, and
Speak Truth to Power: Voices from Beyond the Dark. A Distinguished
Professor at Duke University, human rights activist, and contributor
to major papers and journals across the world, he has received numer-
ous international awards for his poetry, essays, and novels. His latest
work is the memoir *Feeding on Dreams: Confessions of an Unrepentant*

Exile, a sequel to *Heading South, Looking North*, both of them dedicated to his wife, Angélica.

The Spanish novelist Javier Marías (b. 1951) has published thirteen novels, three collections of short stories, and several volumes of essays. His novels include *Todas las almas / All Souls* (1988), *Corazón tan blanco / A Heart so White* (1992), *Mañana en la batalla piensa en mí / Tomorrow in the Battle Think on Me* (1994), *Negra espalda del tiempo / Dark Back of Time* (1998), and *Los enamoramientos / The Infatuations* (2013). He is also the translator of various English classics into Spanish, notably *Tristram Shandy*. He has held academic posts in Spain, the United States, and Britain as Lecturer in Spanish Literature at Oxford University.

Hokku

FUKUDA CHIYO-NI (1703-75)

→ ←

BORIS AKUNIN

I think that I understood the meaning of poetry for the first time when I read this *hokku* written by Chiyo, a Japanese poetess of the eighteenth century.

To understand poetry, to be deeply moved by its beauty and force, one needs a key. I felt immediately that there was a mystery in this formula, which sounds so beautiful in Japanese ('*Tonbo-tsuri kefu wa doko made itta yara?*'), but looks devoid of meaning. A dragonfly catcher? Is it a symbol of some kind clear only to a Japanese?

The mystery made me dig deeper and I learned that, no, it wasn't something esoterically Japanese.

Chiyo wrote that poem when her little son died. On writing the *hokku* she became a nun.

In the original there are only seventeen syllables. This masterpiece moves me so much that in homage to it I once wrote a long, long novel. The first volume consists of seventeen chapters and is called *Dragonfly Catcher*. The second volume, *Between the Lines*, is four times thicker and explains the meaning of the first. All in all, it is five hundred pages, and it cannot even remotely compare to Chiyo's miniature. That's what poetry is about.

Hokku

Dragonfly catcher,
Where today
have you gone?

(c. 1740–1775)

➔ ⬅

The Russian philologist, critic, essayist, and translator Boris Akunin (b. Grigory Shalvovich Chkhartishvili, 1956) began publishing detective stories in 1998 and has become one of the most widely read authors in Russia. His Erast Fandorin series of books, full of literary games and allusions, are translated into English by Andrew Bromfield. This translation of Chiyo's *hokku* (later known as a 'haiku') is his own.

Wandrers Nachtlied II

JOHANN WOLFGANG VON GOETHE (1749–1832)

➔ ←

JOHN LE CARRÉ

I chose this poem in part because it is a gem of German lyrical poetry; and in part because the beauty of the German language has long been lost on British ears, and it's high time for a revival. And finally because the 'Nachtlied' is a moving and exquisite contemplation of old age.

Wandrers Nachtlied II	**Wayfarer's Night Song II**
Über allen Gipfeln	Over all the hilltops
Ist Ruh,	is calm.
In allen Wipfeln	In all the treetops
Spürest du	you feel
Kaum einen Hauch;	hardly a breath of air.
Die Vögelein schweigen	The little birds fall silent
in Walde.	in the woods.
Warte nur, balde	Just wait . . . soon
Ruhest du auch.	you'll also be at rest.

(1776)

TRANSLATION BY HYDE FLIPPO

➔ ←

Often billed a spy turned writer, John le Carré (b. David Cornwell, 1931) prefers to describe himself as 'a writer who, when very young, spent a few ineffectual but extremely formative years in British Intelligence'. His many books include the 'Smiley' novels, *The Spy Who Came in from the Cold* (1963), *The Naïve and Sentimental Lover* (1971), *Tinker Tailor Soldier Spy* (1974), and, most recently, *A Delicate Truth* (2013).

Frost at Midnight

SAMUEL TAYLOR COLERIDGE (1772–1834)

→ ←

SEBASTIAN FAULKS

Coleridge was a shambolic man who was too often distracted by drugs and worldly matters to write the poetry his talent warranted. Yet for a moment here everything is held in perfect poise. Alone, late at night, a man and his sleeping child . . . The warmth of the flickering fire keeps at bay the freezing night, and in the silence Coleridge travels back into his life. He touches on a Wordsworthian sense of the spirit that impels and runs through all natural things. Then, with a surge of paternal love, he projects himself into his son's future: the regrets and constraints of his own life shall underwrite the joy and liberation of his child's.

The clinching first word of the last stanza, 'Therefore', resonates like the church bell of Ottery St Mary, where Coleridge was reared. The language achieves a Shakespearean beauty and command, with the impudent repetition of 'quiet' in the final line.

The force of a father's love has enabled the poet to find his true and immortal voice. It is desperately poignant, both in its eloquence and in the fact that such moments were so few for Coleridge.

I read this poem at my daughter's christening.

Frost at Midnight

The Frost performs its secret ministry,
Unhelped by any wind. The owlet's cry
Came loud – and hark, again! loud as before.
The inmates of my cottage, all at rest,
Have left me to that solitude, which suits
Abstruser musings: save that at my side
My cradled infant slumbers peacefully.
'Tis calm indeed! so calm, that it disturbs
And vexes meditation with its strange
And extreme silentness. Sea, hill, and wood,
This populous village! Sea, and hill, and wood,
With all the numberless goings-on of life,
Inaudible as dreams! the thin blue flame
Lies on my low-burnt fire, and quivers not;
Only that film, which fluttered on the grate,
Still flutters there, the sole unquiet thing.
Methinks, its motion in this hush of nature
Gives it dim sympathies with me who live,
Making it a companionable form,
Whose puny flaps and freaks the idling Spirit
By its own moods interprets, every where
Echo or mirror seeking of itself,
And makes a toy of Thought.

                              But O! how oft,
How oft, at school, with most believing mind,
Presageful, have I gazed upon the bars,
To watch that fluttering *stranger*! and as oft
With unclosed lids, already had I dreamt

Of my sweet birth-place, and the old church-tower,
Whose bells, the poor man's only music, rang
From morn to evening, all the hot Fair-day,
So sweetly, that they stirred and haunted me
With a wild pleasure, falling on mine ear
Most like articulate sounds of things to come!
So gazed I, till the soothing things, I dreamt,
Lulled me to sleep, and sleep prolonged my dreams!
And so I brooded all the following morn,
Awed by the stern preceptor's face, mine eye
Fixed with mock study on my swimming book:
Save if the door half opened, and I snatched
A hasty glance, and still my heart leaped up,
For still I hoped to see the *stranger's* face,
Townsman, or aunt, or sister more beloved,
My play-mate when we both were clothed alike!

Dear Babe, that sleepest cradled by my side,
Whose gentle breathings, heard in this deep calm,
Fill up the interspersèd vacancies
And momentary pauses of the thought!
My babe so beautiful! it thrills my heart
With tender gladness, thus to look at thee,
And think that thou shalt learn far other lore,
And in far other scenes! For I was reared
In the great city, pent 'mid cloisters dim,
And saw nought lovely but the sky and stars.
But *thou*, my babe! shalt wander like a breeze
By lakes and sandy shores, beneath the crags
Of ancient mountain, and beneath the clouds,
Which image in their bulk both lakes and shores

And mountain crags: so shalt thou see and hear
The lovely shapes and sounds intelligible
Of that eternal language, which thy God
Utters, who from eternity doth teach
Himself in all, and all things in himself.
Great universal Teacher! he shall mould
Thy spirit, and by giving make it ask.

Therefore all seasons shall be sweet to thee,
Whether the summer clothe the general earth
With greenness, or the redbreast sit and sing
Betwixt the tufts of snow on the bare branch
Of mossy apple-tree, while the nigh thatch
Smokes in the sun-thaw; whether the eave-drops fall
Heard only in the trances of the blast,
Or if the secret ministry of frost
Shall hang them up in silent icicles,
Quietly shining to the quiet Moon.

(1798)

→ ←

The novelist Sebastian Faulks (b. 1953) made his name with his historical French trilogy, *The Girl at the Lion d'Or* (1989), *Birdsong* (1993), and *Charlotte Gray* (1998). His dozen other novels include *A Fool's Alphabet* (1992), *Human Traces* (2005), *Engleby* (2007) and *A Week in December* (2009). He has also published authorised sequels to Ian Fleming's James Bond cycle in *Devil May Care* (2008) and P. G. Wodehouse's Jeeves and Wooster series in *Jeeves and the Wedding Bells* (2013).

Character of the Happy Warrior

WILLIAM WORDSWORTH (1770–1850)

→ ←

HAROLD EVANS

In 1988, the family of Sir Denis Hamilton (1918–1988) asked if I'd speak these verses at his memorial service. When I read them again, I knew that I'd be in trouble holding back tears. Hamilton was an idealist whose ideals, in the end, were betrayed. Stanza after stanza, I was moved by lines so very appropriate to his life as the soldier I never knew and the journalist who was my mentor for some twenty years.

At twenty-two he was a junior officer shoulder-deep in the waves at Dunkirk, trying to save the one hundred sixty survivors of the thousand-strong battalion of his beloved Durham Light Infantry that he'd taken into battle. In his forties, he was the editorial genius of the *Sunday Times*. 'What knowledge can perform' he was diligent to learn, determined to apply an unashamed curiosity not simply to events but also to the elevation of public standards, taste and enlightenment. He remained the King's Scout he'd been as a boy in Middlesbrough. The commonest question he had for me, as the editor who succeeded him, was 'Have you done your good deed for the day, Harold?' He meant it. His moral being was his prime concern.

Character of the Happy Warrior

Who is the happy Warrior? Who is he
That every man in arms should wish to be?
 – It is the generous Spirit, who, when brought
Among the tasks of real life, hath wrought
Upon the plan that pleased his childish thought:
Whose high endeavours are an inward light
That makes the path before him always bright;
Who, with a natural instinct to discern
What knowledge can perform, is diligent to learn;
Abides by this resolve, and stops not there,
But makes his moral being his prime care;
Who, doomed to go in company with Pain,
And Fear, and Bloodshed, miserable train!
Turns his necessity to glorious gain;
In face of these doth exercise a power
Which is our human nature's highest dower:
Controls them and subdues, transmutes, bereaves
Of their bad influence, and their good receives:
By objects, which might force the soul to abate
Her feeling, rendered more compassionate;
Is placable – because occasions rise
So often that demand such sacrifice;
More skilful in self-knowledge, even more pure,
As tempted more; more able to endure,
As more exposed to suffering and distress;
Thence, also, more alive to tenderness.
 – 'Tis he whose law is reason; who depends
Upon that law as on the best of friends;
Whence, in a state where men are tempted still
To evil for a guard against worse ill,

And what in quality or act is best
Doth seldom on a right foundation rest,
He labours good on good to fix, and owes
To virtue every triumph that he knows:
 – Who, if he rise to station of command,
Rises by open means; and there will stand
On honourable terms, or else retire,
And in himself possess his own desire;
Who comprehends his trust, and to the same
Keeps faithful with a singleness of aim;
And therefore does not stoop, nor lie in wait
For wealth, or honours, or for worldly state;
Whom they must follow; on whose head must fall,
Like showers of manna, if they come at all:
Whose powers shed round him in the common strife,
Or mild concerns of ordinary life,
A constant influence, a peculiar grace;
But who, if he be called upon to face
Some awful moment to which Heaven has joined
Great issues, good or bad for human kind,
Is happy as a Lover; and attired
With sudden brightness, like a Man inspired;
And, through the heat of conflict, keeps the law
In calmness made, and sees what he foresaw;
Or if an unexpected call succeed,
Come when it will, is equal to the need:
 – He who, though thus endued as with a sense
And faculty for storm and turbulence,
Is yet a Soul whose master-bias leans
To homefelt pleasures and to gentle scenes;

Sweet images! which, wheresoe'er he be,
Are at his heart; and such fidelity
It is his darling passion to approve;
More brave for this, that he hath much to love: –
'Tis, finally, the Man, who, lifted high,
Conspicuous object in a Nation's eye,
Or left unthought-of in obscurity, –
Who, with a toward or untoward lot,
Prosperous or adverse, to his wish or not –
Plays, in the many games of life, that one
Where what he most doth value must be won:
Whom neither shape or danger can dismay,
Nor thought of tender happiness betray;
Who, not content that former worth stand fast,
Looks forward, persevering to the last,
From well to better, daily self-surpast:
Who, whether praise of him must walk the earth
For ever, and to noble deeds give birth,
Or he must fall, to sleep without his fame,
And leave a dead unprofitable name –
Finds comfort in himself and in his cause;
And, while the mortal mist is gathering, draws
His breath in confidence of Heaven's applause:
This is the happy Warrior; this is he
That every man in arms should wish to be.

(1806)

→ ←

Sir Harold Evans (b. 1928) is regarded as Britain's foremost postwar
newspaper editor, above all for his stewardship of *The Sunday Times*

from 1967 to 1981. Since moving to New York in 1984 he has been the founding editor of *Condé Nast Traveler*, president and publisher of the Random House group, and held several executive roles in journalism, currently editor-at-large for Reuters. He has also published books ranging from autobiography and journalism manuals to American history, notably *The American Century* (1998).

Surprised by Joy

WILLIAM WORDSWORTH (1770–1850)

➔ ←

HOWARD JACOBSON

This is not a poem of hot grief. Yes, it begins with cruel immediacy, the poet turning to share spontaneous joy with someone no longer there to share joy with, but he does not evoke his 'heart's best treasure' with agonising vividness, nor does his voice falter with sorrow commensurate to the loss. If anything, the voice is strong and collected, and it's in that collectedness that the anguish lies, the scrupulousness of the remorse, the almost pedantic examination of how much memory owes to love, and how exacting the computation must always be. 'How could I forget thee . . . through what power even for the *least* division of an hour.' By a more forgiving, less vigilant account he hasn't forgotten her at all. Did he not, in a moment of faithful love, turn to share his joy with her? But it's not enough to remember her as though she's there; loyalty demands he must never forget, not for that smallest division of time, the fact that she isn't and never again will be. This is the terrifying, unconsoling paradox of remembrance, and it breaks the heart.

Surprised by Joy

Surprised by joy – impatient as the Wind
I turned to share the transport – Oh! with whom
But Thee, deep buried in the silent tomb,
That spot which no vicissitude can find?
Love, faithful love, recalled thee to my mind –
But how could I forget thee? – Through what power,
Even for the least division of an hour,
Have I been so beguiled as to be blind
To my most grievous loss? – That thought's return
Was the worst pang that sorrow ever bore,
Save one, one only, when I stood forlorn,
Knowing my heart's best treasure was no more;
That neither present time, nor years unborn
Could to my sight that heavenly face restore.

(1815)

→ ←

Howard Jacobson (b. 1942) won the Man Booker Prize in 2010
for *The Finkler Question*. His other novels include *Zoo Time* (2012),
an apocalyptic comedy about the end of reading and *J* (2014), which
was shortlisted for the Man Booker Prize. He has also published
five works of nonfiction, most recently *Whatever It Is, I Don't Like
It* (2011), a collection of his columns for the (London) *Independent*.

Last Sonnet

JOHN KEATS (1795-1821)

→ ←

KENNETH LONERGAN

Like the other two or three poems I can actually recite by heart, 'Last Sonnet' (or 'Bright Star,' as many know it today) was read to me by my friend, the painter Patricia Broderick.

Keats knew he was dying when he wrote 'Bright Star', aged twenty-three, onboard a ship he was taking to Italy in the hope that the warmer climate would save his life – which of course it could not. The trip and his illness marked the end of his romance with Fanny Brawne.

Even as Keats stands in awe at the star's majesty and mystery – 'in lone splendour hung aloft the night' – and even as he imagines what it would be like to be a star, looking down on the beautiful Earth he is leaving, even then that's not what he wishes for. No, he wants the star's perpetual span of life, so that he can be 'Pillow'd on my fair love's ripening breast / To feel forever its soft fall and swell / Awake for ever in a sweet unrest . . .'

Long before my friend Patsy herself died, the content and context of this poem invariably reduced me to a useless puddle of tears. And it still does, not because it reminds me of her, but because of the miracle that enables another human being to carry me back in time and over the ocean with nothing more than a sequence of words, onto the deck of a ship where I am really and truly looking at the stars with someone else's eyes, intimately connected with his thoughts, understanding in my heart something of his feelings.

Last Sonnet

Bright star, would I were steadfast as thou art –
Not in lone splendour hung aloft the night
And watching, with eternal lids apart,
Like nature's patient, sleepless Eremite,
The moving waters at their priestlike task
Of pure ablution round earth's human shores,
Or gazing on the new soft-fallen mask
Of snow upon the mountains and the moors –
No – yet still stedfast, still unchangeable,
Pillow'd upon my fair love's ripening breast,
To feel for ever its soft fall and swell,
Awake for ever in a sweet unrest,
Still, still to hear her tender-taken breath,
And so live ever – or else swoon to death.

(1818–1819)

→ ←

The playwright, screenwriter, and director Kenneth Lonergan (b. 1962) wrote and directed the films *You Can Count On Me* (2000) and *Margaret* (2011). His stage credits include *This Is Our Youth* (1996), *The Waverley Gallery* (2000), *Lobby Hero* (2001), *The Starry Messenger* (2009), and *Medieval Play* (2012). Among Lonergan's other screenplays are *Analyse This* (1999) and Martin Scorsese's *Gangs of New York* (2002), which was cowritten with Jay Cocks and Steven Zaillian.

Extract from
The Masque of Anarchy

PERCY BYSSHE SHELLEY (1792–1822)

➔ ◂

DAVID EDGAR

News of the Peterloo Massacre of 16 August 1819 – during which British cavalry killed fifteen and injured up to seven hundred men and women at a Manchester rally for parliamentary reform – reached Shelley in Italy three weeks later. The resultant ninety-one-stanza poem was not to be published for thirteen years.

The title refers not to the anarchy of protest but to the brutality of the politicians who put it down ('I met Murder on the way – / He had a mask like Castlereagh'). The parade of Murder and his allies (Anarchy itself mounted 'like Death in the Apocalypse') is met by a 'maniac maid' whose name is Hope but 'looked more like Despair.' The second half of the poem consists of her speech, imagining the gathering of a 'great assembly' whose nonviolent resistance to armed tyranny anticipates Thoreau and Gandhi.

No one who has ever been at, or been inspired by, a great demonstration can fail to be moved by Hope's final call for the people to rise 'in unvanquishable number'. The last line is even more devastating. Shelley has established a variation in his four-line stanza pattern, adding an occasional, unexpected, third-rhyming fifth line. Earlier, the device emphasises brutality and starvation. At the end, it celebrates something very different.

The Masque of Anarchy XC-XCI

'And these words shall then become
Like Oppression's thundered doom
Ringing through each heart and brain,
Heard again – again – again –

'Rise like Lions after slumber
In unvanquishable number –
Shake your chains to earth like dew
Which in sleep had fallen on you –
Ye are many – they are few.'

(1819)

→ ←

More than sixty plays by David Edgar (b. 1948) have been performed around the world on stage, radio, and TV. They include *Destiny* (1976), *Maydays* (1983), *The Shape of the Table* (1990), *Albert Speer* (2000), *The Continental Divide* (2003), *Playing with Fire* (2005), *Written on the Heart* (2011), and *If Only* (2013), as well as an adaptation of Dickens, *The Life and Adventures of Nicholas Nickleby* (1980). Formerly Professor of Playwriting at the University of Birmingham, he has also written several books about theatre, including *The Second Time as Farce* (1988) and *How Plays Work* (2009).

I Am

JOHN CLARE (1793–1864)

→ ←

KEN LOACH

So many poems can touch you. Which one to choose? A war poem? Who could read Wilfred Owen's words and remain unmoved? In 'Disabled', he describes a soldier, both legs gone, waiting in his wheel-chair to be put to bed.

Then there are poems of mourning and loss. Goethe's 'The Erl-King', where a child is taken from the arms of his father as he rides through the night, captures the acute, shocking pain of sudden be-reavement. In another vein, there are Christina Rossetti's poems of lost love: 'Remember me when I am gone away . . .'

Shelley is one of the many poets who have written of the struggle of the common people to end oppression. After the Peterloo Massacre, he wrote in 'Men of England':

The seed ye sow, another reaps:
The wealth ye find, another keeps.

The sadness comes from hopes betrayed so many times, despite the courage of those who resist. But I have to choose one. John Clare wrote of the countryside with great affection but spent his last years in an asylum. This poem tells of a man reduced to nothingness – bereft, abandoned, beyond tears. The desperation of Clare's words leaves you weeping for all who share his plight.

I Am

I am – yet what I am, none cares or knows,
My friends forsake me like a memory lost: –
I am the self-consumer of my woes; –
They rise and vanish in oblivion's host,
Like shades in love and death's oblivion lost;
And yet I am! and live with shadows tost

Into the nothingness of scorn and noise, –
Into the living sea of waking dreams,
Where there is neither sense of life nor joys,
But the vast shipwreck of my life's esteems;
And e'en the dearest – that I loved the best –
Are strange – nay, rather stranger than the rest.

I long for scenes where man hath never trod;
A place where woman never smiled or wept;
There to abide with my Creator, God,
And sleep as I in childhood sweetly slept,
Untroubling and untroubled where I lie;
The grass below – above the vaulted sky.

(1844–1845)

→ ←

After a brief spell in the theatre, Ken Loach (b. 1936) was recruited by the BBC in 1963 as a television director. This launched a long career directing films for television and the cinema, from *Cathy Come Home* (1966) and *Kes* (1969) to *Land and Freedom* (1995), *Sweet Sixteen* (2002), *The Wind That Shakes The Barley* (2006), *The Angels' Share* (2012), *The Spirit of '45* (2013) and *Jimmy's Hall* (2014).

Of the Terrible
Doubt of Appearances

WALT WHITMAN (1819–1892)

→ ←

STEPHEN FRY

For some reason, the blubbiest poem for me has always been Whitman's 'Of The Terrible Doubt of Appearances'. It's Uncle Walt at his most perfect, I think. The strangely jerky parenthetical hiccups in the middle all build into an ending that never fails to choke me.

Of the Terrible Doubt of Appearances
Of the terrible doubt of appearances,
Of the uncertainty after all, that we may be deluded,
That may-be reliance and hope are but speculations
      after all,
That may-be identity beyond the grave is a beautiful
      fable only,
May-be the things I perceive, the animals, plants, men,
      hills, shining and flowing waters,
The skies of day and night, colors, densities, forms,
      May-be these are (as doubtless they are) only

apparitions, and the real something has yet to be
known;
(How often they dart out of themselves, as if to con-
found me and mock me!
How often I think neither I know, nor any man knows,
aught of them,)
May-be seeming to me what they are (as doubtless
they indeed but seem) as from my present point
of view, And might prove (as of course they
would) naught of what they appear, or naught
anyhow, from entirely changed points of view;
To me, these and the like of these are curiously
answer'd by my lovers, my dear friends,
When he whom I love travels with me or sits a long
while holding me by the hand,
When the subtle air, the impalpable, the sense that
words and reason hold not, surround us and
pervade us,
Then I am charged with untold and untellable wisdom,
I am silent, I require nothing further,
I cannot answer the question of appearances or that
of identity beyond the grave,
But I walk or sit indifferent, I am satisfied,
He ahold of my hand has completely satisfied me.

(1860)

→ ←

The writer, actor, and TV and radio presenter Stephen Fry (b. 1957)
has published four novels, several nonfiction works, three volumes of
autobiography and a guide to writing poetry, *The Ode Less Travelled*

(2005). He has appeared in some thirty movies, notably *Wilde* (1997), directed *Bright Young Things* (2003) and voiced all seven of the *Harry Potter* audiobooks. His many TV appearances include *Blackadder* (1986–8), and his most recent stage role was as Malvolio at the Globe Theatre and in London's West End in 2012, and on Broadway in 2013.

Remember

CHRISTINA ROSSETTI (1830–1894)

➜ ←

ROBERT FISK

As I write these words, I prepare for my next fraught journey back to Baghdad, back to the suicide bombers and the throat-cutters and the fast-firing Americans. And through the veil of Iraqi tears, I will draw more portraits of suffering and pain and greed and occasional courage and I wonder if, when I eventually leave this vast chamber of horrors, I will try to emulate the advice of the only poem that always moves me to tears, Christina Rossetti's 'Remember':

> Better by far you should forget and smile
>> Than that you should remember and be sad.

JULIAN FELLOWES

I don't have a very good ear for poetry or for music either, really. As a general rule, I am more influenced by prose and I must be one of the few who think Dorothy Wordsworth's description of the daffodils considerably more effective than her brother William's poem. But I am moved by 'Remember', perhaps because I became aware of it when my family was essentially waiting for my mother to die of the cancer that had been shutting her down for two years. I had not seen much of death before that point, other than a pair of legs under a crashed car on the M1, and the enormity of the change, the idea of saying good-bye forever, seemed for a while to engulf me. In the end, my mother's departure was peaceful and un-horrid, and there was a comfort in that, but I do recall that sense of disloyalty in the early months, when I would find myself laughing at a party and suddenly remember that she was gone and my poor father was alone, and Rossetti's words did resonate with me, expressing, as they do, a feeling that my late and so-lamented parent would have thoroughly endorsed. As it happens, I don't know to whom the poem was originally addressed, but I suppose, in the end, great poetry, like great art, is not about anyone in particular because it is about everyone.

Remember

Remember me when I am gone away,
    Gone far away into the silent land;
    When you can no more hold me by the hand,
Nor I half turn to go yet turning stay.
Remember me when no more day by day
    You tell me of our future that you plann'd:
    Only remember me; you understand
It will be late to counsel then or pray.
Yet if you should forget me for a while
    And afterwards remember, do not grieve:
    For if the darkness and corruption leave
    A vestige of the thoughts that once I had,
Better by far you should forget and smile
    Than that you should remember and be sad.

(1862)

→ ←

These thoughts of the veteran war reporter Robert Fisk (b. 1946), Middle East correspondent for *The Times* and *Independent* for more than thirty years, are the closing words of his book *The Great War for Civilisation: The Conquest of the Middle East* (2005).

The writer, actor and director Julian Fellowes (b. Cairo, 1949) is best known as the creator of the award-winning TV series *Downton Abbey* and for his Oscar-winning screenplay for Robert Altman's 2002 film *Gosford Park*. As well as appearing as an actor on TV and the West End stage, and in films such as *Tomorrow Never Dies* (1997), he has published several novels and wrote the stage version of *Mary Poppins* (2004). He was created a life peer in 2011.

After Great Pain

EMILY DICKINSON (1830–1886)

→ ←

DOUGLAS KENNEDY

In the United States we are in love with one of the more specious words in the modern lexicon: closure. This word is employed whenever the spectre of tragedy has cast its shadow on a life. 'I need to achieve closure' is a common lament in the wake of a profound grief. Yet lurking behind this proclamation is the equally spurious belief that the horrors which life can wreak upon us – and which we can also wreak upon ourselves – can be eventually placed in a box, put on a shelf and shut away forever.

Emily Dickinson's masterpiece of a poem points up one of the reasons why her work so endures and so resonates with the modern consciousness. It speaks directly to the heart of the matter. It doesn't flinch in the face of human contradiction and the way we all try to negotiate the worst that life can throw at us. And within its diamond-hard craftsmanship – its lyrical economy, its imagistic precision – Dickinson not only speaks volumes about the shadowland of despair that is the price of being given the gift of life, but also reminds us of one of the central truths with which we all grapple: to live is to harbour so many profound losses.

After Great Pain

After great pain a formal feeling comes –
The Nerves sit ceremonious like Tombs;
The stiff Heart questions – was it He that bore
And Yesterday – or Centuries before?

The Feet, mechanical, go round
A Wooden way
Of Ground, or Air, or Ought,
Regardless grown,
A Quartz contentment, like a stone.

This is the Hour of Lead
Remembered if outlived,
As Freezing persons recollect the Snow –
First Chill – then Stupor – then the letting go.

(c. 1864)

＋ ＋

Douglas Kennedy (b. 1955) has published ten novels (translated into twenty-two languages), three of which, *The Dead Heart* (1994), *The Big Picture* (1997) and *The Woman in the Fifth* (2007), have been made into films. He has also written three works of nonfiction, *Beyond the Pyramids: Travels in Egypt* (1988), *In God's Country: Travels in the Bible Belt* (1989) and *Chasing Mammon* (1992).

Extract from *Peer Gynt*

HENRIK IBSEN (1828–1906)

→ ←

KENNETH BRANAGH

In Christopher Fry's verse translation of Ibsen's *Peer Gynt*, there is a sermon by a pastor towards the end of the play. Peer listens while the priest tells the story (in verse) of a young man from the mountains who mutilates himself to avoid joining the army and losing his sweetheart. The sermon is the brief story of the young man's life, and in this version – a fine poet's translation of a fine poet – it always makes me cry.

From *Peer Gynt*
And now, when the soul has gone its way to judgment,
And the flesh reposes here like an empty pod,
Now, dear friends, we have a word to say
About this dead man's journeyings on earth.
        He wasn't rich, or of great understanding;
His voice was small, he had no manly bearing;
He gave his opinions shyly, uncertainly,
Was scarcely master in his own house.
In church, he walked like someone who would ask
Permission to sit there among the others.

He came from Gudbrands valley, as you know.
When he settled here he was hardly more than a boy;
And you all remember how, up to the last,
He always kept his right hand in his pocket.

This right hand in the pocket was the thing
That impressed the man's image on one's mind;
And also the uneasiness, the shy
Reticence when he walked into the room.

But though he preferred to go his quiet way,
And though he seemed a stranger here among us,
You all know (though he tried hard to conceal it)
There were only four fingers on the hand he hid. –

I remember, on a morning many years ago,
A meeting at Lunde to enroll recruits.
It was war-time. Everybody was discussing
The country's ordeal, and what lay ahead.

I stood watching. Sitting behind the table
Was the Captain, the parish clerk and some N.C.O.s.
They took the measure of one boy after another,
Swore them in and took them for the army.
The room was full, and outside you could hear
The crowd of young men laughing in the yard.

Then a name was shouted. Another lad came forward,
Looking as pale as the snow on a glacier.
They called him nearer; he approached the table;
A piece of rag was tied round his right hand.
He gasped, swallowed, groped about for words,
But couldn't speak, in spite of the Captain's order.
However, his cheeks burning, stammering still
And speaking very quickly, he managed at last
To mumble something about an accidental

Slip of a scythe that sheared his finger off.

       Silence fell on the room, as soon as he had said it.
Men exchanged looks, and their lips tightened.
They all stoned the boy with silent stares.
He felt the hail-storm, but he didn't see it.
The Captain, an elderly, grey-haired man, stood up,
Spat, pointed a finger and said Get out!

       And the boy went. Everyone drew aside
So that he had to run the gauntlet between them.
He got as far as the door, then took to his heels
Up and off, across the fields and hillside,
Scrambling on over the shale and rocks,
To where his home was, high on the mountainside.

       Six months later he came to live down here
With a mother, a newborn child, and his wife-to-be.
He leased a plot of ground way up on the hill
Where the derelict land joins the parish of Lom.
He married as soon as he could; put up a house;
Ploughed the stony ground, and made his way,
As the waving gold of his little fields bore witness.
At church he kept his right hand in his pocket,
But back at home no doubt those nine fingers
Did the work of other people's ten. –

       One spring a flood carried it all away.
Only their lives were spared. Everything lost,
He set to work to make another clearing,
And by the autumn smoke rose up again
From a hillside farm, this time better sheltered.
Sheltered? Yes, from flood; but not from glaciers.
Two years later it all lay under the snow.

       Yet not even an avalanche could crack his courage.

He dug, and cleared, and carted away the debris,
And before the next winter-snows came drifting
His little house was built for the third time.

He had three sons, three fine vigorous boys;
They should go to school, but the school was a long way off.
They could only reach the end of the valley road
By going through a narrow, precipitous pass.
What did he do? The eldest looked after himself
As best he could, and where the track dropped steeply
This man roped him round to give him support;
The others he bore in his arms and on his back.

He toiled like this, year after year, until
The sons were men. Time, you would have thought,
To get some return. Three prosperous gentlemen
In the New World have managed to forget
Their Norwegian father and those journeys to school.

His horizon was narrow. Apart from the few
Who were nearest to him, nothing else existed.
The ringing words that rouse other men's hearts
Meant nothing to him, more than a tinkle of bells.
Mankind, the fatherland, the highest ambitions
Of men, were only misty figures to him.

But he had humility, humility, this man;
And after that call-up day he always carried
The shame of the verdict, as surely as his cheeks
Carried the burn of shyness, and his four
Fingers hid in his pocket. – An offender
Against the laws of the land? Yes, indeed!
But there's one thing that shines above the law,
As truly as the bright tent of Glitretind
Has even higher peaks of cloud above it.

He was a poor patriot. To State
And Church, an unproductive tree. But there
On the brow of the hill, within the narrow
Circle of family, where his work was done,
There he was great, because he was himself.
He matched up to the living sounds he was born with.
His life was like a music on muted strings.

     So peace be with you, silent warrior,
Who strove and fell in the peasant's little war!
We won't try to probe the ways of his heart.
That's for his Maker, not for us, to do.
But I can hold this hope, with little doubt;
He is not maimed now as he stands before his God.

(1867)

TRANSLATION BY CHRISTOPHER FRY

→ ←

Sir Kenneth Branagh (b. 1960) is one of Britain's most successful actors and directors in film, television and theatre. In addition to his acclaimed cinema adaptations of Shakespeare's plays, he has also directed and/or acted in films such as *Valkyrie* (2008), *Thor* (2010), *My Week with Marilyn* (2011) and *Jack Ryan: Shadow Recruit* (2014). He has had huge TV success with his BAFTA-winning portrayal of Wallander and has received five Academy Award nominations in five different categories.

Requiem

ROBERT LOUIS STEVENSON (1850–94)

➣ ⬿

CHRISTOPHER BUCKLEY

Probably unnecessary to explain why this poem almost always brings tears to my eyes. It speaks for itself. In April 2008, I recited it from memory at St Patrick's Cathedral, New York City, in front of 2,200 people at the memorial mass for the repose of my father's soul. It was a particular favourite of his, and well describes him. On that occasion I managed not to cry, having rehearsed in private until my ducts had run dry. But I did slightly clutch at the penultimate line.

Requiem
Under the wide and starry sky,
Dig the grave and let me lie.
Glad did I live and gladly die,
    And I laid me down with a will.

This be the verse you 'grave for me:
Here he lies where he longed to be;
Home is the sailor, home from sea,
    And the hunter home from the hill.

(1880–1884)

→ ←

Once a speechwriter to President George H. W. Bush, which resulted in his first comic novel, *The White House Mess* (1986), Christopher Buckley (b. 1952) has published numerous satirical novels including *Thank You for Smoking* (1994), which was filmed by Jason Reitman; *Little Green Men* (1999); *No Way to Treat a First Lady* (2002); *Florence of Arabia* (2004); *Boomsday* (2007); *Supreme Courtship* (2008); and *They Eat Puppies, Don't They?* (2012). He is also the author of *Losing Mum and Pup* (2009), a memoir about his parents, William and Pat Buckley, and *But Enough About You*, a collection of essays.

The Remorseful Day

A. E. HOUSMAN (1859–1936)

➜ ⬅

JOE KLEIN

Both my parents passed away in the winter of 2011–12. They had been together for eighty-six years, since their first day of kindergarten. My father lasted only a few weeks after my mother went; his will to live sapped visibly the moment I told him she was gone. 'Is it definite?' he asked.

At the same time, my wife and I were in the midst of a major television-watching project: all thirty-three episodes of *Inspector Morse* in chronological order. There are no twelve-step programmes for British-mystery lovers. We're addicted, and Morse – irascible, imbibing, extravagantly literate and mysteriously first-nameless (it turned out to be 'Endeavour') – was a favourite.

We came to the final episode a week after my father died and I began to blub – decorously, blotting the corner of my eye with an index finger, but in full blub all the same – when Morse, played by the brilliant John Thaw, recited the Housman. It was triply poignant. Morse was dying. Thaw was near death himself. My parents had just passed away. When I later read the poem, I was slightly disappointed. 'Ensanguining' the skies seemed a bit much . . . until I read it aloud, and the funereal metre reasserted itself. I miss Morse, Thaw and, of course, my parents. But the poem remains, a reminder of grief so pure that it can also cleanse.

The Remorseful Day
Ensanguining the skies
How heavily it dies
Into the west away;
Past touch and sight and sound
Not further to be found,
How hopeless under ground
Falls the remorseful day.

(c. 1896)

→ ←

Originally as Anonymous, Joe Klein (b. 1946) wrote *Primary Colors* (1996), subsequently filmed by Mike Nichols. A political columnist for *Time* magazine since 2003, he is a member of the Council on Foreign Relations and a former Guggenheim Fellow.

The Wind, One Brilliant Day

ANTONIO MACHADO (1875–1939)

→ ←

ROBERT BLY

This is a poem about the many losses that everybody, men and women, go through in life. The older you get, the more gardens you have abandoned. What else is there to do? Now you see how many old friends are gone, and how things didn't turn out the way you had hoped.

The Wind, One Brilliant Day
The wind, one brilliant day, called
to my soul with an aroma of jasmine.

'In return for the odor of my jasmine,
I'd like all the odor of your roses.'

'I have no roses, all the flowers
in my garden are dead.'

'Well then, I'll take the waters of the fountains,
and the withered petals and the yellow leaves.'

The wind left. And I wept. And I said to myself:
'What have you done with the garden that was entrusted to you?'

(C. 1903)

TRANSLATION BY ROBERT BLY

→ ←

The poet, author, and activist Robert Bly (b. 1926) is best known for his 1990 work *Iron John: A Book About Men*, which spent sixty-two weeks on the *New York Times* bestseller list. An influential editor of poetry magazines and anthologies, he has also published some twenty volumes of poetry, sixteen volumes of translation and nine works of nonfiction.

Orpheus. Eurydice. Hermes

RAINER MARIA RILKE (1875–1926)

→ ←

COLM TÓIBÍN

What is strange is how much coiled emotion a single declaratory sentence can have. In this translation, Mitchell trusts the words. They will do the work. 'Nothing else was red' stops you, suggests that this is a real landscape, rather than one which is mythological, or that it is oddly and vividly both, and all the more powerful and present for that. Then, the elaborate description of landscape begins again to be followed once more by a single sentence: 'Down this path they were coming.' The poem is filled with hardness. Orpheus is 'mute, impatient, looking straight ahead.' He is desperate to get her back, it is not just a dream or an ancient myth, it is you now. Death comes here as both unforgiving and relentless, but it is also an active state. 'She was filled with her own vast death' has the power to console as much as to suggest completion, finality. She will be too busy, too distracted to notice who is ahead. The man who loved her will be merely 'someone or other'; he will have been too impatient. The dead will not come back, but the words will, and the words will be filled with sad wisdom as the woman who was so loved will move into eternity, or nothing much, or perhaps nothing at all, in ways that are 'uncertain, gentle, and without impatience'.

Orpheus. Eurydice. Hermes

That was the deep uncanny mine of souls.
Like veins of silver ore, they silently
moved through its massive darkness. Blood welled up
among the roots, on its way to the world of men,
and in the dark it looked as hard as stone.
Nothing else was red.

There were cliffs there,
and forests made of mist. There were bridges
spanning the void, and that great gray blind lake
which hung above its distant bottom
like the sky on a rainy day above a landscape.
And through the gentle, unresisting meadows
one pale path unrolled like a strip of cotton.

Down this path they were coming.

In front, the slender man in the blue cloak –
mute, impatient, looking straight ahead.
In large, greedy, unchewed bites his walk
devoured the path; his hands hung at his sides,
tight and heavy, out of the falling folds,
no longer conscious of the delicate lyre
which had grown into his left arm, like a slip
of roses grafted onto an olive tree.
His senses felt as though they were split in two:
his sight would race ahead of him like a dog,
stop, come back, then rushing off again
would stand, impatient, at the path's next turn, –
but his hearing, like an odor, stayed behind.

Sometimes it seemed to him as though it reached
back to the footsteps of those other two
who were to follow him, up the long path home.
But then, once more, it was just his own steps' echo,
or the wind inside his cloak, that made the sound.
He said to himself, they had to be behind him;
said it aloud and heard it fade away.
They had to be behind him, but their steps
were ominously soft. If only he could
turn around, just once (but looking back
would ruin this entire work, so near
completion), then he could not fail to see them,
those other two, who followed him so softly:

The god of speed and distant messages,
a traveler's hood above his shining eyes,
his slender staff held out in front of him,
and little wings fluttering at his ankles;
and on his left arm, barely touching it: she.

A woman so loved that from one lyre there came
more lament than from all lamenting women;
that a whole world of lament arose, in which
all nature reappeared: forest and valley,
road and village, field and stream and animal;
and that around this lament-world, even as
around the other earth, a sun revolved
and a silent star-filled heaven, a lament-
heaven, with its own, disfigured stars – :
So greatly was she loved.

But now she walked beside the graceful god,
her steps constricted by the trailing graveclothes,
uncertain, gentle, and without impatience.
She was deep within herself, like a woman heavy
with child, and did not see the man in front
or the path ascending steeply into life.
Deep within herself. Being dead
filled her beyond fulfillment. Like a fruit
suffused with its own mystery and sweetness,
she was filled with her vast death, which was so new,
she could not understand that it had happened.

She had come into a new virginity
and was untouchable; her sex had closed
like a young flower at nightfall, and her hands
had grown so unused to marriage that the god's
infinitely gentle touch of guidance
hurt her, like an undesired kiss.

She was no longer that woman with blue eyes
who once had echoed through the poet's songs,
no longer the wide couch's scent and island,
and that man's property no longer.

She was already loosened like long hair,
poured out like fallen rain,
shared like a limitless supply.

She was already root.

And when, abruptly,
the god put out his hand to stop her, saying,
with sorrow in his voice: He has turned around – ,
she could not understand, and softly answered
Who?

                    Far away,
dark before the shining exit-gates,
someone or other stood, whose features were
unrecognizable. He stood and saw
how, on the strip of road among the meadows,
with a mournful look, the god of messages
silently turned to follow the small figure
already walking back along the path,
her steps constricted by the trailing graveclothes,
uncertain, gentle, and without impatience.

(1904)

TRANSLATION BY STEPHEN MITCHELL

→ ←

The Irish novelist Colm Tóibín (b. 1955) has also published short sto-
ries, plays, journalism and poetry. He is the winner of the 2011 Irish
PEN Award and currently is the Irene and Sidney B. Silverman Pro-
fessor of the Humanities at Columbia University. His novels include
The Blackwater Lightship (1999), *Brooklyn* (2009), *The Testament of
Mary* (2012), *Nora Webster* (2014); his most recent work of criticism
is *New Ways to Kill Your Mother: Writers and their Families* (2012).

Ithaka

CONSTANTINE P. CAVAFY (1863–1933)

→ ←

WALTER SALLES

Someone once told me: 'Don't ask the way of those who know it, you might not get lost.'

Ithaka
As you set out for Ithaka
hope the voyage is a long one,
full of adventure, full of discovery.
Laistrygonians and Cyclops,
angry Poseidon – don't be afraid of them:
you'll never find things like that on your way
as long as you keep your thoughts raised high,
as long as a rare excitement
stirs your spirit and your body.
Laistrygonians and Cyclops,
wild Poseidon – you won't encounter them
unless you bring them along inside your soul,
unless your soul sets them up in front of you.

Hope the voyage is a long one.
May there be many a summer morning when,
with what pleasure, what joy,
you come into harbors seen for the first time;
may you stop at Phoenician trading stations
to buy fine things,
mother of pearl and coral, amber and ebony,
sensual perfume of every kind –
as many sensual perfumes as you can;
and may you visit many Egyptian cities
to gather stores of knowledge from their scholars.

Keep Ithaka always in your mind.
Arriving there is what you are destined for.
But do not hurry the journey at all.
Better if it lasts for years,
so you are old by the time you reach the island,
wealthy with all you have gained on the way,
not expecting Ithaka to make you rich.

Ithaka gave you the marvelous journey.
Without her you would not have set out.
She has nothing left to give you now.

And if you find her poor, Ithaka won't have fooled you.
Wise as you will have become, so full of experience,
you will have understood by then what these Ithakas mean.

(1911)

TRANSLATION BY EDMUND KEELEY AND PHILIP SHERRARD

→ ←

The films of the Brazilian director Walter Salles (b. 1956) include *Terra Estrangeira / Foreign Land* (1996*), Central do Brasil / Central Station* (1998), *Abril Despedaçado / Behind the Sun* (2001), *Diarios de Motocicleta / The Motorcycle Diaries* (2004), *Dark Water* (2005), *Linha de Passe* (2008) and *On The Road* (2012).

At Castle Boterel

THOMAS HARDY (1840–1928)

➜ ←

ALAN HOLLINGHURST

This is one of several great poems written by Hardy after the death of his first wife, in which he and she reappear as their youthful selves in phantom form, haunting charged places in the Wessex landscape. Since this is also the landscape of most of Hardy's novels, and he had stopped writing fiction a decade earlier, the poem seems an elegy too for himself and for his own long career.

It's now forty years since I first read it, and though its rhythms are as familiar to me as those of a favourite piece of music, the idiosyncratic wording and dexterous rhyming keep it as alive as any stubborn ghost, the clinching dimeter of each stanza paying off overwhelmingly in the last line of all.

At Castle Boterel

As I drive to the junction of lane and highway,
  And the drizzle bedrenches the waggonette,
I look behind at the fading byway,
  And see on its slope, now glistening wet,
     Distinctly yet

Myself and a girlish form benighted
  In dry March weather. We climb the road
Beside a chaise. We had just alighted
  To ease the sturdy pony's load
          When he sighed and slowed.

What we did as we climbed, and what we talked of
  Matters not much, nor to what it led, –
Something that life will not be balked of
  Without rude reason till hope is dead,
          And feeling fled.

It filled but a minute. But was there ever
  A time of such quality, since or before,
In that hill's story? To one mind never,
  Though it has been climbed, foot-swift, foot-sore,
          By thousands more.

Primaeval rocks form the road's steep border,
  And much have they faced there, first and last,
Of the transitory in Earth's long order;
  But what they record in colour and cast
          Is – that we two passed.

And to me, though Time's unflinching rigour,
  In mindless rote, has ruled from sight
The substance now, one phantom figure
  Remains on the slope, as when that night
          Saw us alight.

I look and see it there, shrinking, shrinking,
  I look back at it amid the rain
For the very last time; for my sand is sinking,
  And I shall traverse old love's domain
        Never again.

(1912)

→ ←

The novelist and poet Alan Hollinghurst (b. 1954) won the 2004 Man Booker Prize for his novel *The Line of Beauty*. His other works include *The Swimming Pool Library* (1988), *The Stranger's Child* (2011) and translations of two plays by Racine.

The Voice

THOMAS HARDY (1840–1928)

→ ←

SEAMUS HEANEY

I can't honestly say that I break down when I read 'The Voice', but when I get to the last four lines the tear ducts do congest a bit. The poem is one of several Thomas Hardy wrote immediately after the death of his first wife in late November 1912, hence the poignancy of his dating it 'December 1912'. Hardy once described this group of memorial poems as 'an expiation', acknowledging his grief and remorse at the way he had neglected and hurt the one 'who was all to me . . . at first, when our day was fair'. What renders the music of the poem so moving is the drag in the voice, as if there were sinkers on many of the lines. But in the final stanza, in that landscape of falling leaves, wind and thorn, and the woman calling, there is a banshee note that haunts 'long after it is heard no more'.

The Voice
Woman much missed, how you call to me, call to me,
Saying that now you are not as you were
When you had changed from the one who was all to me,
But as at first, when our day was fair.

Can it be you that I hear? Let me view you, then,
Standing as when I drew near to the town
Where you would wait for me: yes, as I knew you then,
Even to the original air-blue gown!

Or is it only the breeze in its listlessness
Traveling across the wet mead to me here,
You being ever dissolved to wan wistlessness,
Heard no more again far or near?

Thus I; faltering forward,
Leaves around me falling,
Wind oozing thin through the thorn from norward,
And the woman calling.

(1912)

> <

With twelve volumes of original poems to his name, and several books
of critical essays, translations and drama, Seamus Heaney (1939–
2013) was awarded the 1995 Nobel Prize for Literature.

Adlestrop

EDWARD THOMAS (1878–1917)

→ ←

SIMON WINCHESTER

I suppose I should stop kidding myself and admit that I'll probably never go back to live in England. I'm an American citizen now. When I reached that famous fork in the woods, I took the road less travelled (Robert Frost and Edward Thomas were friends) and ended up on a weary farm in Massachusetts. That doesn't stop a certain yearning though: whenever I see *The Last of the Summer Wine*, or hear the Queen at Christmas-time, I long for England, only to go back and find that what I longed for has all but vanished.

I left home in 1966, by chance the year they closed Adlestrop station, a quiet two-platform halt on the Oxford to Worcester main line. The old railway system then began its own long decline: stations closed, lines torn up, engines sent for scrap. There was something infinitely special and terribly English about a half-deserted country railway station on a blissful summer's day. I listen to this deceptively slight poem, immediately smell creosote and gillyflowers, can hear the waiting-room clock, the clank of signal wires – but then have to blink my eyes, every time. This is the England that I loved; I weep for its passing.

Adlestrop

Yes. I remember Adlestrop –
The name, because one afternoon
Of heat the express-train drew up there
Unwontedly. It was late June.

The steam hissed. Someone cleared his throat.
No one left and no one came
On the bare platform. What I saw
Was Adlestrop – only the name

And willows, willow-herb, and grass,
And meadowsweet, and haycocks dry,
No whit less still and lonely fair
Than the high cloudlets in the sky.

And for that minute a blackbird sang
Close by, and round him, mistier,
Farther and farther, all the birds
Of Oxfordshire and Gloucestershire.

(1914)

➔ ←

Once a geologist, Simon Winchester (b. 1944) spent almost thirty years as a foreign correspondent for *The Guardian* and other newspapers in various countries until the handover of Hong Kong in 1997, when he became a full-time writer. He has written twenty-five nonfiction books, dealing with such topics as the Oxford English Dictionary, the origins of geology, China, the Atlantic Ocean and, most recently, the uniting of the United States.

The Soldier

RUPERT BROOKE (1887–1915)

➔ ←

HUGH BONNEVILLE

Like many schoolchildren, I was introduced to this sonnet when studying the poets of the First World War. The graphic bitterness of Siegfried Sassoon and Wilfred Owen, we were instructed, was to be contrasted with the naïve patriotism of Rupert Brooke.

Brooke's view of death and his love of country is that of a clear-eyed young man who, like the hundreds of thousands of others who rushed to join up, felt confident of purpose and of victory within months, entirely innocent of what was to come. I won't judge him for that.

Every time I watch the movie *Gladiator* this poem comes to mind. Like the recurring motif of Maximus's hand brushing the wheat of his fields as he heads for his waiting family, 'The Soldier', for me, is ultimately about belonging. It's about coming home.

And it's not the notion of death with honour or pride in motherland that moves me, it's the simple phrase 'laughter, learnt of friends' that gets me every time. An image of happiness shared, in a land at peace.

With the privilege of hindsight I find it is as pitiful as it is beautiful in its evocation of contentment.

The Soldier

If I should die, think only this of me:
    That there's some corner of a forcign field
That is for ever England. There shall be
    In that rich earth a richer dust concealed;
A dust whom England bore, shaped, made aware,
    Gave, once, her flowers to love, her ways to roam,
A body of England's, breathing English air,
    Washed by the rivers, blest by suns of home.

And think, this heart, all evil shed away,
    A pulse in the eternal mind, no less
    Gives somewhere back the thoughts by England given;
Her sights and sounds; dreams happy as her day;
    And laughter, learnt of friends; and gentleness,
    In hearts at peace, under an English heaven.

(1914)

→ ←

The actor Hugh Bonneville (b. 1963) is perhaps best known for his portrayal of Lord Grantham in television's *Downton Abbey*, and for the Olympics mockumentary series *Twenty Twelve*. His feature films include *Notting Hill* (1999), *Mansfield Park* (1999), *Iris* (2001), *The Monuments Men* (2014) and *Paddington* (2014).

During Wind and Rain

THOMAS HARDY (1840–1928)

→ ←

KEN FOLLETT

I read this as a schoolboy, and even then I was overwhelmed by its melancholy. Half a century of rereading has shown me how clever it is. The rhyming scheme – ABCBCDA – and the stanza form are unique, as far as I know. In each verse, the first five lines swing like a pop song, showing us a family engaged in a merry project: singing, gardening, picnicking. Moving house is vividly evoked with the simple image of clocks on the lawn. But every stanza is a sucker punch. In the last two lines of each the rhythm falters, and decay and death are evoked until the end, when we realise that the poet is standing in a rain-wet graveyard, looking at the tombstones, and everyone in that happy family is now dead.

During Wind and Rain

> They sing their dearest songs –
> He, she, all of them – yea,
> Treble and tenor and bass,
>   And one to play;
> With the candles mooning each face. . . .
>   Ah, no; the years O!
> How the sick leaves reel down in throngs!

They clear the creeping moss –
Elders and juniors – aye,
Making the pathways neat
    And the garden gay;
And they build a shady seat. . . .
    Ah, no; the years, the years;
See, the white storm-birds wing across!

They are blithely breakfasting all –
Men and maidens – yea,
Under the summer tree,
    With a glimpse of the bay,
While pet fowl come to the knee. . . .
    Ah, no; the years O!
And the rotten rose is ript from the wall.

They change to a high new house,
He, she, all of them – aye,
Clocks and carpets and chairs
    On the lawn all day,
And brightest things that are theirs. . . .
    Ah, no; the years, the years;
Down their carved names the rain-drop ploughs.

                    (1917)

          ❧ ❧

The Welsh-born novelist Ken Follett (b. 1949) has sold more than 130 million books worldwide. His first bestseller was *Eye of the Needle* (1978), a spy story set during the Second World War. In 1989 *The Pillars of the Earth* marked a radical change; a novel about building a cathedral in the Middle Ages, it has sold more than nineteen million copies in many languages. His latest project is the Century trilogy, three historical novels telling the story of the twentieth century through the eyes of five families: *Fall of Giants* (2010), *Winter of the World* (2012) and *Edge of Eternity* (2014).

Dulce et Decorum Est

WILFRED OWEN (1893–1918)

➔ ◆

CHRISTOPHER HITCHENS

Christopher Hitchens was one of the first to contribute to this anthology, in an e-mail just five days before his death in December 2011.

In the foreword to his 2000 volume of literary criticism, *Unacknowledged Legislation: Writers in the Public Sphere*, Hitchens writes: 'Most of Owen's poetry was written or "finished" in the twelve months before his life was thrown away in a futile action on the Sambre-Meuse canal, and he only published four poems in his lifetime . . . But he has conclusively outlived all the jingo versifiers, blood-bolted Liberal politicians, garlanded generals and other supposed legislators of the period. He is the most powerful single rebuttal of Auden's mild and sane claim that "Poetry makes nothing happen".'

Dulce et Decorum Est

Bent double, like old beggars under sacks,
Knock-kneed, coughing like hags, we cursed through sludge,
Till on the haunting flares we turned our backs
And towards our distant rest began to trudge.
Men marched asleep. Many had lost their boots

But limped on, blood-shod. All went lame; all blind;
Drunk with fatigue; deaf even to the hoots
Of tired, outstripped Five-Nines that dropped behind.

Gas! GAS! Quick, boys! – An ecstasy of fumbling,
Fitting the clumsy helmets just in time;
But someone still was yelling out and stumbling,
And flound'ring like a man in fire or lime . . .
Dim, through the misty panes and thick green light,
As under a green sea, I saw him drowning.

In all my dreams, before my helpless sight,
He plunges at me, guttering, choking, drowning.

If in some smothering dreams you too could pace
Behind the wagon that we flung him in,
And watch the white eyes writhing in his face,
His hanging face, like a devil's sick of sin;
If you could hear, at every jolt, the blood
Come gargling from the froth-corrupted lungs,
Obscene as cancer, bitter as the cud
Of vile, incurable sores on innocent tongues, –
My friend, you would not tell with such high zest
To children ardent for some desperate glory,
The old Lie: Dulce et decorum est
Pro patria mori.

(1917–1918)

→ ←

For four decades Christopher Hitchens (1949–2011) was one of the most prominent and controversial writers and journalists of his time, publishing twelve books and five collections of essays. British-born but US-resident, with dual nationality, he was a regular columnist for *Vanity Fair*. His 2007 polemic *God Is Not Great* reached number one on the *New York Times* best-seller list.

God's World

EDNA ST VINCENT MILLAY (1892–1950)

→ ←

PATRICK STEWART

I had never believed the New England fall could possibly be as beautiful as people claimed. And then one morning after breakfast I left my friends' house in South Salem, New York State, having arrived in the dark the previous evening. I walked two hundred yards along the lane and broke down helplessly weeping with the never-before-seen beauty and grandeur of it all.

God's World
O world, I cannot hold thee close enough!
　　Thy winds, thy wide grey skies!
　　Thy mists, that roll and rise!
Thy woods, this autumn day, that ache and sag
And all but cry with colour! That gaunt crag
To crush! To lift the lean of that black bluff!
World, World, I cannot get thee close enough!

Long have I known a glory in it all,
　　But never knew I this;
　　Here such a passion is

As stretcheth me apart, – Lord, I do fear
Thou'st made the world too beautiful this year;
My soul is all but out of me, – let fall
No burning leaf; prithee, let no bird call.

(1917)

→ ←

Sir Patrick Stewart (b. 1940) has graduated via many Shakespearean and other classical roles for the Royal Shakespeare Company and London's National Theatre to international fame as Captain Picard in *Star Trek: The Next Generation* and Professor Xavier in the *X Men* series. Amid more than ninety film and TV credits on both sides of the Atlantic, his recent returns to the stage in London's West End and on Broadway include the title role in *Macbeth* (2007), Claudius in *Hamlet* (2008), Shylock in *The Merchant of Venice* (RSC, 2011) and Vladimir in Samuel Beckett's *Waiting for Godot* (2009), revived on Broadway with Harold Pinter's *No Man's Land* in 2013.

Everyone Sang

SIEGFRIED SASSOON (1886–1967)

→ ←

BARRY HUMPHRIES

This much-anthologised poem remains deeply affecting, evoking as it does a picture of First World War soldiers in a moment of emotional release.

Everyone Sang
Everyone suddenly burst out singing;
And I was filled with such delight
As prisoned birds must find in freedom,
Winging wildly across the white
Orchards and dark-green fields; on – on – and out of sight.

Everyone's voice was suddenly lifted;
And beauty came like the setting sun:
My heart was shaken with tears; and horror
Drifted away . . . O, but Everyone
Was a bird; and the song was wordless; the singing will never be
    done.

(1919)

The Australian actor, writer, artist and comedian Barry Humphries (b. 1934) is best known for his stage and TV alter egos Dame Edna Everage and Sir Les Patterson. He has also starred in films from *The Adventures of Barry McKenzie* (1972) to *The Hobbit: An Unexpected Journey* (2012) and written numerous books on a wide range of subjects.

Last Poems: XL

A. E. HOUSMAN (1859–1936)

→ ←

ANDREW MOTION

'Make them laugh, make them cry, make them wait': that's what Dickens used to say about the structure of his novels. 'Make them laugh, make them cry, bring on the dancing girls': that's what Philip Larkin said about the ordering of poems in his slim collections. The wish (the impulse, the need, the requirement) to make an audience cry is conspicuous in both cases, and it's always been high on my list of requirements as a reader. As I get older, the requirement is more and more easily met.

Why is this? Because our hearts grow softer as the years click past? Perhaps. But also because we feel the sadness of the creatures (and our fellow human beings) more keenly. And because we can see the dark at the end of the tunnel more and more clearly. Almost the whole of Shakespeare (comedies and tragedies) makes tears pour down my face. So do large chunks of Wordsworth and Tennyson. And almost everything by Hardy and Edward Thomas . . . Some days I only have to *think* of particular poems to start going. And every day I only have to think about A. E. Housman's poem . . . well, there are several I could mention. But while I can still see the keyboard let me choose number XL in *Last Poems*: 'Tell me not here, it needs not saying . . .'

RICHARD DAWKINS

This poem is not from *A Shropshire Lad* but it has the same hauntingly wistful air. I knew it by heart as a boy in love – not with any particular girl but with the idea of being in love, and especially the tragedy of lost love. Much later, when I organised the funeral of my friend and mentor the evolutionary biologist W. D. Hamilton in New College chapel, his sister chose the poem for her reading. I was not surprised to learn that it was one of Bill's favourites, because he had long brought to my mind the melancholy protagonist of *A Shropshire Lad*. In my book *River Out of Eden*, I had earlier quoted – actually misquoted from memory – the last verse, when I wanted to convey the indifferent callousness of Darwinian natural selection, noted by Darwin himself. The politician Douglas Jay, who also loved Housman, pointed out my misquotation to me, and I gratefully corrected it in later printings of the book. Here is the correct version:

> For nature, heartless, witless nature,
> Will neither care nor know.

DNA neither cares nor knows. DNA just is. And we dance to its music.

Last Poems: XL
Tell me not here, it needs not saying,
  What tune the enchantress plays
In aftermaths of soft September
  Or under blanching mays,
For she and I were long acquainted
  And I knew all her ways.

On russet floors, by waters idle,
  The pine lets fall its cone;
The cuckoo shouts all day at nothing
  In leafy dells alone;
And traveller's joy beguiles in autumn
  Hearts that have lost their own.

On acres of the seeded grasses
  The changing burnish heaves;
Or marshalled under moons of harvest
  Stand still all night the sheaves;
Or beeches strip in storms for winter
  And stain the wind with leaves.

Possess, as I possessed a season,
  The countries I resign,
Where over elmy plains the highway
  Would mount the hills and shine,
And full of shade the pillared forest
  Would murmur and be mine.

For nature, heartless, witless nature,
  Will neither care nor know
What stranger's feet may find the meadow
  And trespass there and go,
Nor ask amid the dews of morning
  If they are mine or no.

(1922)

→ ←

The poet, novelist, and biographer Sir Andrew Motion (b. 1952) was Britain's Poet Laureate from 1999 to 2009. As well as several volumes of poetry, he has published biographies of John Keats and Philip Larkin. He is also president of the Campaign to Protect Rural England.

The many publications of the ethologist and evolutionary biologist Richard Dawkins (b. 1941) include *The Selfish Gene* (1976), *The Extended Phenotype* (1982), *The Blind Watchmaker* (1986), *River Out of Eden* (1995), *The God Delusion* (2006) and a memoir, *An Appetite for Wonder* (2013). Professor for Public Understanding of Science at Oxford University from 1995 to 2008, he is an emeritus fellow of New College, Oxford. In 2013 he led *Prospect* magazine's list of the world's Top 100 living thinkers.

God Wills It

GABRIELA MISTRAL (1889–1957)

→ ←

JEREMY IRONS

I first came across this poem thirty years ago in New York, where I included it in a lunchtime reading I did at St Bartholomew's on Park Avenue. It is, I think, the poem that of all those I read I find the hardest to get through; it stirs very deep emotions within me, not at any particular line, but in the relentless and naked passion that imbues the poem throughout. The love that generates such emotion is unequivocal, takes no prisoners, and is perhaps the love I am, or yearn to be, part of.

God Wills It
I
Earth will turn against you
If your soul betrays my soul.
A shudder of anguish
will run through the waters.
The world has been brighter
since you made me yours,
when we stood silent
by a flowering thorn,

and love's fragrance
pierced us like the thorn.
But earth will send forth vipers
against you if you betray my soul;
I will break my barren knees
no child sits upon.
Christ will die in my heart,
and the door of my house
will break the beggar's knocking hand
and turn the suffering woman away.

II

Every kiss your mouth gives
reaches my ears,
for the deep places of the earth
echo me your words.
The dust of the pathways
holds the scent of your footsoles,
and through the mountains
I track you like a deer.
The clouds above my house
show me the woman you love.
Sneak like a thief to kiss her
in the darkness under earth,
but when you tilt her chin up,
you'll see my tearstained face.

III

God will keep the sun from you
if you don't walk beside me.
God won't let you drink

if I don't tremble on the water.
He won't let you sleep, except
in the deep nest of my hair.

IV

If you let go from me you crush my soul
even in the moss of the road;
hunger and thirst gnaw at you
on every hill and plain,
and wherever you go, sunset
will bleed my wounds.
And I slip from your tongue
though you call another woman,
and I stick like the taste
of brine in your throat,
and whether you hate or praise or plead,
to me you cry, to me alone.

V

If you go and die far from me,
you'll hold out your hollowed hand
for ten years underground,
to catch my tears,
feeling the trembling
of the suffering flesh,
until my bones crumble
into dust on your face.

(1922)

TRANSLATION BY URSULA K. LE GUIN

Jeremy Irons (b. 1948) has played many classical and contemporary roles onstage, starred in TV series from *Brideshead Revisited* (1981) to *The Borgias* (2011) and films from *The French Lieutenant's Woman* (1981) to *Margin Call* (2011). He won an Academy Award for his portrayal of Claus von Bülow in *Reversal of Fortune* (1990).

Out of Work

KENNETH H. ASHLEY (1887–?)

→ ←

FELIX DENNIS

Some time ago, I bought part of the library of the late novelist J. B. Priestley. In the pages of one of his books, *Up Hill and Down Dale* by an obscure poet, Kenneth H. Ashley, published in 1924, I found a slip of paper where Priestley had marked a particular short poem called 'Out of Work'. As soon as I read it, I was transported back almost fifty years to a dingy bedsit in an obscure street (now demolished) in Harrow on the Hill.

It was from here, after quitting Harrow School of Art, that I tramped the local streets looking for work to keep me in Gitanes cigarettes, potato and leek soup, and alcohol. The R&B band I was playing in had work most weeks, but after the fuel bills for the van and the hire-purchase payments on the gear, there was precious little left over to split among the band members and manager.

I eventually found work mowing verges for the council and digging the odd grave (a more skilled occupation than you might think!), but I have never forgotten those far-off days of poverty and hopelessness. I know exactly what Ashley meant when he ended on that shocking six-word line: 'And I wished I were dead.' The only counter to it I can offer those in the same position comes from the pen of a man who never knew want in his life, Winston Churchill: 'If you're going through hell, keep going.'

Easy advice to give but hard to swallow.

Out of Work

Alone at the shut of the day was I,
With a star or two in a frost cleared sky,
And the byre smell in the air.

I'd tramped the length and breadth of the fen,
But never a farmer wanted men;
Naught doing anywhere.

A great calm moon rose back of the mill,
And I told myself it was God's will
Who went hungry and who went fed.

I tried to whistle; I tried to be brave,
But the new ploughed fields smelt dank as the grave;
And I wished I were dead.

(1924)

→ ←

In 1971, as co-editor of *Oz* magazine, Felix Dennis (1947–2014) was imprisoned by the British government at the end of the longest conspiracy trial in English history, during which he recorded a single with John Lennon to raise money for a legal defence fund. Following his subsequent acquittal by the High Court of Appeal, Dennis went on in 1973 to found his own magazine-publishing company. He turned to poetry only in his mid-fifties, and became a popular performance poet, with several best-selling volumes to his name.

All the Pretty Horses

ANONYMOUS

→ ←

CARL BERNSTEIN

I had to really dig deep here – past Shakespeare's sonnets, Blake, Whitman, Keats . . . the canon. And finally I got down to this lullaby that I sang to my children from their birth.

All the Pretty Horses
Hush-by, Don't you cry
Go to sleep a little baby
When you wake you shall find
All the pretty little horses

Blacks and bays, dapples and grays
Coach and six a little horses
When you wake you shall find
All the pretty little horses

Hush-by, Don't you cry
Go to sleep a little baby
When you wake you shall find
All the pretty little horses

(FIRST IN PRINT 1925)

→ ←

Since his celebrated partnership with Bob Woodward for the *Washington Post* on the Nixon presidency and the Watergate scandal, which resulted in *All The President's Men* (1974) and other books, Carl Bernstein (b. 1944) has written biographies of Pope John Paul II (*The Abuse of Power*, with Marco Politi, 1996) and Hillary Rodham Clinton (*A Woman in Charge,* 2007). He has also published a memoir of his parents, *Loyalties* (1989).

The Cool Web

ROBERT GRAVES (1895–1985)

→ ←

JOHN SUTHERLAND

I first came across this poem as an undergraduate. The most inefficient, but wonderfully enthusing, university teacher I've ever known, G. S. Fraser, was pursuing a long, quixotic campaign to draw notice to Robert Graves as the greatest lyric poet of the century. As cultish attention to The Movement [a group of other 1950s British poets] monopolised attention, his voice was drowned out.

Fraser failed. But he converted me. 'The Cool Web' articulates the poignant sense that, whatever one gains intellectually, one loses more. The sentiment is familiar enough from those who know their Wordsworth, and Auden put it into chillier form in 'Their Lonely Betters':

> As I listened from a beach-chair in the shade
> To all the noises that my garden made,
> It seemed to me only proper that words
> Should be withheld from vegetables and birds.

It's cleverer but – in that term of approbation we loved in the 1960s – less 'felt.'

Graves, it seems to me, touches a deeper chord. There is always, in his mature poetry, the still-throbbing scar tissue of a survivor of the 'war called great' ('the inward scream, the duty to run mad', as he put it). Poetry, I think, is the only thing that can make linguistics – that driest of sciences – 'moving'.

I read 'The Cool Web' in the 'madness' (as Graves prophesied) of late life, with a distant gesture of gratitude to G. S. Fraser and a moistening of the eye.

The Cool Web

Children are dumb to say how hot the day is,
How hot the scent is of the summer rose,
How dreadful the black wastes of evening sky,
How dreadful the tall soldiers drumming by.

But we have speech, to chill the angry day,
And speech, to dull the rose's cruel scent,
We spell away the overhanging night,
We spell away the soldiers and the fright.

There's a cool web of language winds us in,
Retreat from too much joy or too much fear:
We grow sea-green at last and coldly die
In brininess and volubility.

But if we let our tongues lose self-possession,
Throwing off language and its watery clasp
Before our death, instead of when death comes,
Facing the wide glare of the children's day,
Facing the rose, the dark sky and the drums,
We shall go mad, no doubt, and die that way.

(1940)

→ ←

John Sutherland (b. 1938) is Lord Northcliffe Professor Emeritus of Modern English Literature at University College, London. Among his many books are the Stanford *Companion to Victorian Fiction* (1989, rev. 2009), a series of 'puzzles in classic fiction' entitled *Is Heathcliff a Murderer?* (1996), *Can Jane Eyre Be Happy?* (1997) and *Who Betrays Elizabeth Bennett?* (1999), as well as the authorised life of Stephen Spender (2004), *Lives of the Novelists* (2011) and two volumes of autobiography, *Last Drink to LA* (2001), *The Boy Who Loved Books* (2007) and *Jumbo,* an 'unauthorised' biography of Jumbo the Elephant (2014).

The Broken Tower

HART CRANE (1899–1932)

➤ ◀

HAROLD BLOOM

This poem is Hart Crane's farewell to the art of poetry, which was his life. I do not know another poem like it, despite its packed allusiveness. There are parallels of equal distinction: Donne's 'A Nocturnal upon Saint Lucy's Day', Milton's 'Lycidas', Blake's 'The Mental Traveller', Shelley's 'Ode to the West Wind', Whitman's 'As I Ebb'd with the Ocean of Life'.

Crane desperately needed reassurance that he was still a poet, but it was not forthcoming. His suicide [at the age of thirty-two] perhaps would have come even if he had been persuaded that his great gifts were intact. He had been doom-eager all his life.

The Broken Tower

The bell-rope that gathers God at dawn
Dispatches me as though I dropped down the knell
Of a spent day – to wander the cathedral lawn
From pit to crucifix, feet chill on steps from hell.

Have you not heard, have you not seen that corps
Of shadows in the tower, whose shoulders sway

Antiphonal carillons launched before
The stars are caught and hived in the sun's ray?

The bells, I say, the bells break down their tower;
And swing I know not where. Their tongues engrave
Membrane through marrow, my long-scattered score
Of broken intervals . . . And I, their sexton slave!

Oval encyclicals in canyons heaping
The impasse high with choir. Banked voices slain!
Pagodas, campaniles with reveilles outleaping –
O terraced echoes prostrate on the plain! . . .

And so it was I entered the broken world
To trace the visionary company of love, its voice
An instant in the wind (I know not whither hurled)
But not for long to hold each desperate choice.

My word I poured. But was it cognate, scored
Of that tribunal monarch of the air
Whose thigh embronzes earth, strikes crystal Word
In wounds pledged once to hope, – cleft to despair?

The steep encroachments of my blood left me
No answer (could blood hold such a lofty tower
As flings the question true?) – or is it she
Whose sweet mortality stirs latent power? –

And through whose pulse I hear, counting the strokes
My veins recall and add, revived and sure

The angelus of wars my chest evokes:
What I hold healed, original now, and pure . . .

And builds, within, a tower that is not stone
(Not stone can jacket heaven) – but slip
Of pebbles, – visible wings of silence sown
In azure circles, widening as they dip

The matrix of the heart, lift down the eye
That shrines the quiet lake and swells a tower . . .
The commodious, tall decorum of that sky
Unseals her earth, and lifts love in its shower.

(1932)

→ ←

Harold Bloom (b. 1930) is Sterling Professor of the Humanities at the University of Yale. His many publications include *Shakespeare: The Invention of the Human* (1998) and *The Anatomy of Influence* (2011), from which the above introductory words are taken.

Bavarian Gentians

D. H. LAWRENCE (1885–1930)

→ ←

SIMON ARMITAGE

The poem is very melancholy, gloomy even, a twilight poem both literally and metaphorically. But it's a late poem in Lawrence's life, and I think it signals a kind of readiness for whatever might follow, written by someone at ease with his situation and not afraid of that journey into the eternal underworld. The mythology of the poem has also puzzled me – the poet appears ready to witness the violence of Pluto's advances on Persephone, but of course she's also a goddess of spring-time and rebirth . . . The concluding rhyme strikes me as a reinforcement of the poet's desire for personal peace and closure. The poem is so graceful, easy, and apparently effortless.

Bavarian Gentians
Not every man has gentians in his house
in soft September, at slow, sad Michaelmas.

Bavarian gentians, big and dark, only dark
darkening the daytime torch-like with the smoking blueness of
   Pluto's gloom,

ribbed and torch-like, with their blaze of darkness spread blue
down flattening into points, flattened under the sweep of white
   day
torch-flower of the blue-smoking darkness, Pluto's dark-blue
   daze,
black lamps from the halls of Dis, burning dark blue,
giving off darkness, blue darkness, as Demeter's pale lamps give
   off light,
lead me then, lead me the way.

Reach me a gentian, give me a torch!
Let me guide myself with the blue, forked torch of this flower
down the darker and darker stairs, where blue is darkened on
   blueness
even where Persephone goes, just now, from the frosted
   September
to the sightless realm where darkness is awake upon the dark
and Persephone herself is but a voice
or a darkness invisible enfolded in the deeper dark
of the arms Plutonic, and pierced with the passion of dense
   gloom,
among the splendor of torches of darkness, shedding darkness on
   the lost bride and groom.

                                (1933)

➤ ❖

Simon Armitage (b. 1963) has published ten volumes of poetry, in-
cluding *The Not Dead* (2008), *Seeing Stars* (2011) and *Paper Aero-
planes* (2014). His dramatisation of *The Odyssey* was broadcast on
BBC Radio, and his translation of the Middle English classic poem

Sir Gawain and the Green Knight was published in 2007. He has also written over a dozen television films and prose work including two novels and the memoir *All Points North* (1998). Armitage has taught at the University of Leeds, the University of Iowa's Writers' Workshop and Manchester Metropolitan University. He is currently Professor of Poetry at the University of Sheffield.

A Summer Night

W. H. AUDEN (1907–73)

→ ←

WILLIAM BOYD

First of all, and quite simply, this is a really beautiful poem with W. H. Auden at the height of his amazing powers – master rhymer, master imagist. The picture it conjures up is so magical and the metaphor of 'the lion griefs' – the laying of a muzzle on a thigh, that mute sign of trust and affection – is so powerful that the poem is bound to stir emotion.

However, anyone who knows the history of Auden and his poetry will know that this poem refers to an incident that occurred while Auden was a young teacher at a prep school. As someone who went to a prep school myself, I find this poem, for some reason – perhaps because I remember similar summer nights – effortlessly takes me back to my early childhood. Death puts down his book for a second or two and the tear ducts tingle.

A Summer Night
Out on the lawn I lie in bed,
Vega conspicuous overhead
  In the windless nights of June,
As congregated leaves complete
Their day's activity; my feet
  Point to the rising moon.

Lucky, this point in time and space
Is chosen as my working-place,
  Where the sexy airs of summer,
The bathing hours and the bare arms,
The leisured drives through a land of farms
  Are good to a newcomer.

Equal with colleagues in a ring
I sit on each calm evening
  Enchanted as the flowers
The opening light draws out of hiding
With all its gradual dove-like pleading,
  Its logic and its powers:

That later we, though parted then,
May still recall these evenings when
  Fear gave his watch no look;
The lion griefs loped from the shade
And on our knees their muzzles laid,
  And Death put down his book.

Now north and south and east and west
Those I love lie down to rest;
  The moon looks on them all,
The healers and the brilliant talkers,
The eccentrics and the silent walkers,
  The dumpy and the tall.

She climbs the European sky,
Churches and power stations lie
  Alike among earth's fixtures:

Into the galleries she peers
And blankly as a butcher stares
  Upon the marvelous pictures.

To gravity attentive, she
Can notice nothing here, though we
  Whom hunger does not move,
From gardens where we feel secure
Look up and with a sigh endure
  The tyrannies of love:

And, gentle, do not care to know,
Where Poland draws her eastern bow,
  What violence is done,
Nor ask what doubtful act allows
Our freedom in this English house,
  Our picnics in the sun.

Soon, soon, through the dykes of our content
The crumpling flood will force a rent
  And, taller than a tree,
Hold sudden death before our eyes
Whose river dreams long hid the size
  And vigours of the sea.

But when the waters make retreat
And through the black mud first the wheat
  In shy green stalks appears,
When stranded monsters gasping lie,
And sounds of riveting terrify
  Their whorled unsubtle ears,

May these delights we dread to lose,
This privacy, need no excuse
  But to that strength belong,
As through a child's rash happy cries
The drowned parental voices rise
  In unlamenting song.

After discharges of alarm
All unpredicted let them calm
  The pulse of nervous nations,
Forgive the murderer in the glass,
Tough in their patience to surpass
  The tigress her swift motions.

(1933)

→ ←

Born in Ghana (1952), the British writer William Boyd is the author of twelve novels, including the award-winning *A Good Man in Africa* (1981), *An Ice Cream War* (1982), *Any Human Heart* (2002) and *Restless* (2006). His James Bond novel, *Solo*, was published in 2013. Along with several adaptations of his own novels, his screenplays include *Scoop* (1987), *Mister Johnson* (1990) and *The Trench* (1999), which he also directed. His first play, *Longing*, adapted from two Chekhov short stories, opened in London in 2013.

Those Who Are Near Me Do Not Know

RABINDRANATH TAGORE (1861–1941)

→ ←

CHRIS COOPER

This poem speaks to all who have suffered every parent's worst fear: the loss of a child. Even after the first jolting pain becomes the dimmer sorrow you live with every day, a grieving parent still feels deep love and hopeless yearning for that child, even in the company of others, even in the joy of the creative process, even when many years have passed.

The line 'my heart is full with your unspoken words' resonates in a particular way: my son, Jesse, who died on 3 January 2005, was nonverbal, but always able to speak to my heart's core. The poem ends with a line that is grounded in truth; the love of family and friends is a conduit to the boundless love I knew when my son was alive.

Those Who Are Near Me Do Not Know

Those who are near me do not know that you are nearer to me
    than they are
Those who speak to me do not know that my heart is full with
    your unspoken words
Those who crowd in my path do not know that I am walking
    alone with you

They who love me do not know that their love brings you to my heart.

(1930s)

→ ←

The actor Chris Cooper (b. 1951) has appeared in such films as *American Beauty* (1999), *The Bourne Identity* (2002), *Seabiscuit* (2003), *Syriana* (2005), *Capote* (2005), *The Kingdom* (2007), *Breach* (2007), *The Town* (2010) and *August: Osage County* (2013). He won both the Academy Award and Golden Globe Award for Best Supporting Actor for his performance in *Adaptation* (2002).

Let My Country Awake

RABINDRANATH TAGORE (1861–1941)

→ ←

SALIL SHETTY

I have known this poem since my earliest childhood. Millions of Indian schoolchildren learn the poem at school. Even if I had not learned it at school, I suspect it would have come to my notice anyway.

Such prolonged and forced exposure might usually lead to a deep antipathy to any poem, however great. In this case, however, Tagore's poem has meant more and more to me as I have read it and reread it over the years.

To be truthful, I rarely tear up when reading poetry. I admit that I reserve my tears for over-the-top Bollywood spectaculars, where the chances of my leaving the cinema with dry eyes are embarrassingly low. This poem – translated from Bengali into English by Tagore himself – is, however, special to me in a different way, a powerful call to action and a declaration of belief in achievable change.

Its final line is a powerful culmination of the pent-up aspirations of the poem: 'Into that heaven of freedom, my Father, let my country awake.' The poem was published in 1910, in an India then still part of the British Raj, but the line seems to me more universal than that. It could just as well read: 'Into that heaven of freedom, my Father, let the world awake.' This poem is about universal aspirations, and I love the pugnacious optimism contained within it.

DAVID PUTTNAM

For some while, I've thought we are nearing a tipping point in the fragility of our planet. If we awaken our senses in time to what might be achieved when we act in the interests of everyone, and seriously embrace these sentiments, we could dramatically change the balance of our world to a point where we achieve freedom and fairness for all.

Let My Country Awake
Where the mind is without fear and the head is held high;
Where knowledge is free;
Where the world has not been broken up into fragments by
    narrow domestic walls;
Where words come out from the depth of truth;
Where tireless striving stretches its arms towards perfection;
Where the clear stream of reason has not lost its way into the
    dreary desert sand of dead habit;
Where the mind is led forward by thee into ever-widening
    thought and action –
Into that heaven of freedom, my Father, let my country awake.

(1930s)

→ ←

The Indian-born human rights activist Salil Shetty (b. 1961) is Secretary General of Amnesty International. He has previously served as director of the United Nations Millennium Campaign and Chief Executive of ActionAid.

David Puttnam (b. 1941) is the producer of such films as *Bugsy Malone* (1976), *The Duellists* (1977), *Midnight Express* (1978), *Chariots of Fire* (1981, winner of four Academy Awards, including Best Picture), *Local Hero* (1983), *The Killing Fields* (1984) and *The Mission* (1986). He served as chairman of Columbia Pictures between 1986 and 1988. Since leaving the film industry in 1998, he has concentrated on public work in such fields as education and the environment. He was created a life peer in 1997.

Extract from *Finnegans Wake*

JAMES JOYCE (1882–1941)

➔ ←

JAMES McMANUS

Finnegans Wake is at least as much prose poem as novel. The speaker here is the River Liffey, dying this drizzly morning into the cold Irish Sea below Howth while recirculating as rain on her headwaters. The Liffey represents Joyce's muse and collaborator – his daughter, Lucia. The seventeen years he spent writing the book were also spent watching her swallowed alive down the maw of schizophrenia. Trying every known treatment to save her, he also transmogrified the punny multilingual patois they spoke together into 628 pages of musical dream-language. When the Nazi occupation of France forced her to be evacuated to asylums out of reach of her family, Joyce lamented, 'I have no idea where my daughter is.' They never saw each other again.

My son, James, died in a mental-health facility, out of reach of my ability to comfort him. He was a guitarist, a point guard, a funny and affectionate brother till his illness overwhelmed him. I don't believe in souls, but there's an abscess in mine where he lives.

The eternal-return seam in *Finnegans Wake* reminds me of Joyce's doomed, saltsick efforts to get on Lucia's wavelength and my own dreams of hugging my son, moananoaning, so bad do I still want to save him, carry him along on my shoulders, begin again.

Extract from *Finnegans Wake*

. . . and weary I go back to you, my cold father, my cold mad father, my cold mad feary father, till the near sight of the mere size of him, the moyles and moyles of it, moananoaning, makes me seasilt saltsick and I rush, my only, into your arms. I see them rising! Save me from those therrble prongs! Two more. Onetwo moremens more. So. Avelaval. My leaves have drifted from me. All. But one clings still. I'll bear it on me. To remind me of. Lff! So soft this morning, ours. Yes. Carry me along, taddy, like you done through the toy fair! If I seen him bearing down on me now under whitespread wings like he'd come from Arkangels, I sink I'd die down over his feet, humbly dumbly, only to washup. Yes, tid. There's where. First. We pass through grass behush the bush to. Whish! A gull. Gulls. Far calls. Coming, far! End here. Us then. Finn, again! Take. Bussoftlhee, mcmemormee! Till thousendsthee. Lps. The keys to. Given! A way a lone a last a loved a long the

[here the Wake *ends, only to re-commence on its opening page, where the sentence continues]*

riverrun, past Eve and Adam's, from swerve of shore to bend of bay, brings us by a commodius vicus of recirculation back to Howth Castle and Environs.

(1939)

➜ ⬅

James McManus (b. 1951) has published two volumes of poetry and four novels, as well as two celebrated books about poker, *Positively Fifth Street* (2003) and *Cowboys Full: The Story of Poker* (2009). He has written for publications from *The New Yorker* and *Esquire* to the *New York Times* and teaches writing and literature at the School of the Art Institute of Chicago.

In Memory of W. B. Yeats

W. H. AUDEN (1907–1973)

→ ←

SALMAN RUSHDIE

This great poem, written as the shadow of approaching war fell across Europe, magnificently demands that poetry look horror in the eye and still insist on beauty, still 'persuade us to rejoice'. It's the last couplet that makes Auden's highest claim for the power of art, and, especially when spoken aloud, moves me to tears.

In Memory of W. B. Yeats
I
He disappeared in the dead of winter:
The brooks were frozen, the airports almost deserted,
And snow disfigured the public statues;
The mercury sank in the mouth of the dying day.
What instruments we have agree
The day of his death was a dark cold day.

Far from his illness
The wolves ran on through the evergreen forests,
The peasant river was untempted by the fashionable quays;
By mourning tongues
The death of the poet was kept from his poems.

But for him it was his last afternoon as himself,
An afternoon of nurses and rumours;
The provinces of his body revolted,
The squares of his mind were empty,
Silence invaded the suburbs,
The current of his feeling failed; he became his admirers.

Now he is scattered among a hundred cities
And wholly given over to unfamiliar affections,
To find his happiness in another kind of wood
And be punished under a foreign code of conscience.
The words of a dead man
Are modified in the guts of the living.

But in the importance and noise of to-morrow
When the brokers are roaring like beasts on the floor of the
    Bourse,
And the poor have the sufferings to which they are fairly
    accustomed,
And each in the cell of himself is almost convinced of his
    freedom,
A few thousand will think of this day
As one thinks of a day when one did something slightly unusual.
What instruments we have agree
The day of his death was a dark cold day.

II

You were silly like us; your gift survived it all:
The parish of rich women, physical decay,
Yourself. Mad Ireland hurt you into poetry.
Now Ireland has her madness and her weather still,

For poetry makes nothing happen: it survives
In the valley of its making where executives
Would never want to tamper, flows on south
From ranches of isolation and the busy griefs,
Raw towns that we believe and die in; it survives,
A way of happening, a mouth.

III

Earth, receive an honoured guest:
William Yeats is laid to rest.
Let the Irish vessel lie
Emptied of its poetry.

In the nightmare of the dark
All the dogs of Europe bark,
And the living nations wait,
Each sequestered in its hate;

Intellectual disgrace
Stares from every human face,
And the seas of pity lie
Locked and frozen in each eye.

Follow, poet, follow right
To the bottom of the night,
With your unconstraining voice
Still persuade us to rejoice;

With the farming of a verse
Make a vineyard of the curse,

Sing of human unsuccess
In a rapture of distress;

In the deserts of the heart
Let the healing fountain start,
In the prison of his days
Teach the free man how to praise.

(1940)

→ ←

The Indian-born, US-resident writer Sir Salman Rushdie (b. 1947) is the author of eleven novels, notably the 1981 Booker Prize winner *Midnight's Children*, which also won the Best of the Booker in 2008 and was filmed in 2012. His most recent book is a memoir, *Joseph Anton*.

Lullaby

W. H. AUDEN (1907–1973)

→ ←

SIMON SCHAMA

Tears come to me reading Auden's 'Lullaby' to a lover already asleep because the poem suspends time and the brutality of the world ('1937 when fashionable madmen raise/Their pedantic boring cry') at the moment of unanswerably perfect love. The bed is sheltering redemption and the writer, speaking to the slumbering beloved, registers rapture in the kindness of a loving heart. But this is not the fantastical fancy of poets. The word *human* occurs at the opening and closing of the work: 'Human on my faithless arm' and Nights of insult let you pass/Watched by every human love' and it is the honesty embedded amidst sheets and on the pillow that makes the eyes prick and the heart knock.

SIMON CALLOW

Auden has always been a poet who spoke to me – for me. His eloquence, his directness, his formal skill, his jokes, his music, appealed to me from my early teens; I felt I knew him. Added to which he was very openly and explicitly gay.

I loved 'Funeral Blues' long before it became my personal epitaph in *Four Weddings and a Funeral*, especially its melodramatic refrain of:

> He was my North, my South, my East and West,
> My working week and my Sunday rest,
> My noon, my midnight, my talk, my song;
> I thought that love would last for ever: I was wrong.

But it was 'Lullaby' which moved me to instant tears. It described, in unmistakably erotic terms, a particular state of mind and an experience of the heart, a kind of relationship, which I had not yet known for myself, but all of which, with the uncanny emotional prescience of adolescence, I knew would be mine, soon. The sooner the better.

I still find it impossible to utter out loud or even read to myself the opening two lines without breaking down. The poem is essentially a lullaby, and it is partly the caressing, gently rocking rhythm that makes it so affecting: it is instinct with tenderness, care, boundless benevolence.

> But in my arms till break of day
> Let the living creature lie,
> Mortal, guilty, but to me
> The entirely beautiful.

And in the final couplet the benevolence becomes universal. This is my idea of love; if ever I forget it, Auden is there to remind me.

Lullaby
Lay your sleeping head, my love,
Human on my faithless arm;
Time and fevers burn away
Individual beauty from

Thoughtful children, and the grave
Proves the child ephemeral:
But in my arms till break of day
Let the living creature lie,
Mortal, guilty, but to me
The entirely beautiful.

Soul and body have no bounds:
To lovers as they lie upon
Her tolerant enchanted slope
In their ordinary swoon,
Grave the vision Venus sends
Of supernatural sympathy,
Universal love and hope;
While an abstract insight wakes
Among the glaciers and the rocks
The hermit's carnal ecstasy.

Certainty, fidelity
On the stroke of midnight pass
Like vibrations of a bell,
And fashionable madmen raise
Their pedantic boring cry:
Every farthing of the cost,
All the dreaded cards foretell,
Shall be paid, but from this night
Not a whisper, not a thought,
Not a kiss nor look be lost.

Beauty, midnight, vision dies:
Let the winds of dawn that blow

Softly round your dreaming head
Such a day of welcome show
Eye and knocking heart may bless,
Find the mortal world enough;
Noons of dryness find you fed
By the involuntary powers,
Nights of insult let you pass
Watched by every human love.

(1940)

→ ←

The historian Simon Schama (b. 1945) has published seventeen books, notably *The Embarrassment of Riches: An Interpretation of Dutch Culture in the Golden Age* (1987), *Citizens: A Chronicle of the French Revolution* (1989), *Landscape and Memory* (1995), *Rembrandt's Eyes* (1999), a three-volume *History of Britain* (2000–2) and *Rough Crossings* (2005), the last two of which are among the ten documentary series he has made for BBC Television, most recently *Simon Schama's Shakespeare* (2012) and *The Story of the Jews* (2013).

Having played Mozart in the original 1979 stage production of *Amadeus*, Simon Callow (b. 1949) made his film debut in the 1984 screen version as Emmanuel Schikaneder. Amid numerous TV roles, his forty subsequent screen credits include *Four Weddings and a Funeral* (1994), *Shakespeare in Love* (1998) and *Phantom of the Opera* (2004). His many stage appearances include one-man shows as Dickens and Shakespeare as well as *Waiting for Godot* (2009). Also known as a director of plays, musicals and opera, he has published thirteen books most recently *Being An Actor* (1984), *My Life in Pieces* (2010) and biographies of Oscar Wilde, Charles Laughton and Orson Welles.

If I Could Tell You

W. H. AUDEN (1907–1973)

→ ←

ALEXANDER MCCALL SMITH

'If I Could Tell You' is one of W. H. Auden's most beautiful lyrical poems. Like much of his verse, it may strike the reader as opaque. It is certainly enigmatic, but that is what Auden is talking about here – the difficulty of understanding that which simply *is* and cannot necessarily be explained. Several of the lines are very haunting – 'If we should weep when clowns put on their show' and 'The winds must come from somewhere when they blow' are both examples of this. I never tire of reading this poem: it is for me an experience that is very similar to listening to a particularly beautiful passage of Mozart. I am haunted by this poem.

If I Could Tell You

Time will say nothing but I told you so,
Time only knows the price we have to pay;
If I could tell you I would let you know.

If we should weep when clowns put on their show,
If we should stumble when musicians play,
Time will say nothing but I told you so.

There are no fortunes to be told, although,
Because I love you more than I can say,
If I could tell you I would let you know.

The winds must come from somewhere when they blow,
There must be reasons why the leaves decay;
Time will say nothing but I told you so.

Perhaps the roses really want to grow,
The vision seriously intends to stay;
If I could tell you I would let you know.

Suppose the lions all get up and go,
And the brooks and soldiers run away;
Will Time say nothing but I told you so?
If I could tell you I would let you know.

(c. 1940)

→ ←

Born in Zimbabwe in 1948, Alexander McCall Smith was educated there and in Scotland. He enjoyed a distinguished career as a professor of medical law at the University of Edinburgh. In 2005 he left the university to concentrate on his writing, and is now the author of more than sixty books, including the *The No. 1 Ladies' Detective Agency* series, the *44 Scotland Street* series, *The Sunday Philosophy Club* series and *What W. H. Auden Can Do For You* (2013).

Canoe

KEITH DOUGLAS (1920–1944)

→ ←

CLIVE JAMES

Keith Douglas was born to be a classical poet, so it should not be surprising that his beautifully poised poem 'Canoe' was written quite early in his career, before he went off to war and wrote the poems that would make him famous. Yet 'Canoe' is still prodigious for the concentrated pathos of its landscape, the Oxford setting so very like Virgil's *lugetes campos*, the weeping fields. The moment that melts my eyes is towards the end, when the young woman in the canoe is pictured as making her journey alone in the future, because the narrator will not be with her. At that point, the story is already clinched; he has, we think, foreseen his death, although the poem would have remained powerful even if he had got back, grown old and died in bed.

But in a poem that is all grace, the supremely gracious moment is yet to come. Suddenly he becomes a ghost – for decades in my memory, until I corrected it against the text, it was always his ghost, and not his 'spirit' – and he 'kisses her mouth lightly'. By then I can hardly breathe for grief. The grief is personal, of course. My father went away to the war; he, too, was fated never to return, and my mother continued her voyage alone. This great poem could have been written about them, and therefore about me.

Canoe

Well, I am thinking this may be my last
summer, but cannot lose even a part
of pleasure in the old-fashioned art
of idleness. I cannot stand aghast

at whatever doom hovers in the background;
while grass and buildings and the somnolent river,
who know they are allowed to last for ever,
exchange between them the whole subdued sound

of this hot time. What sudden fearful fate
can deter my shade wandering next year
from a return? Whistle and I will hear
and come again another evening, when this boat

travels with you alone toward Iffley:
as you lie looking up for thunder again,
this cool touch does not betoken rain;
it is my spirit that kisses your mouth lightly.

(1940)

→ ←

The Australian-born (1939) author, critic and broadcaster Clive James has lived and worked in the UK since the early 1960s. As well as his autobiographical series *Always Unreliable*, and numerous volumes of criticism, he has published many distinguished volumes of poetry and a translation of Dante's *Divine Comedy* (2013).

My Papa's Waltz

THEODORE ROETHKE (1908–63)

→ ←

STANLEY TUCCI

This poem speaks to me of the adoration that all children of a certain age have for their fathers. The father's life outside the home is hinted at brilliantly through the physical aspects (rough hands, the smell of whiskey), but never clearly defined. There is an aura of danger that these elements carry with them.

One imagines that this small child has been cared for lovingly all day by a sweet and doting mother, has been fed and bathed and just before bedtime the father enters unfed, unbathed and slightly drunk, undoing in an instant any sense of calm domestic order that has been put in place during the day. The father may well be loved or despised by the wife/mother due to his state, we don't know. We just know that the child sees only his happy hero. Innocence is bliss, and something we lose as we age.

My Papa's Waltz
The whiskey on your breath
Could make a small boy dizzy;
But I hung on like death:
Such waltzing was not easy.

We romped until the pans
Slid from the kitchen shelf;
My mother's countenance
Could not unfrown itself.

The hand that held my wrist
Was battered on one knuckle;
At every step you missed
My right ear scraped a buckle.
You beat time on my head
With a palm caked hard by dirt,
Then waltzed me off to bed
Still clinging to your shirt.

(1942)

→ ←

Stanley Tucci (b. 1960) made his screen debut in the 1980s, has earned an Academy Award nomination for his performance in *The Lovely Bones* (2009), and won Golden Globes for playing the title role in HBO's *Winchell* (1998) and as Adolf Eichmann in *Conspiracy* (2001). Onstage, he received a Tony nomination as Johnny in the 2002 Broadway revival of *Frankie and Johnny in the Claire de Lune*. Among his many other film credits are *Billy Bathgate* (1991), *The Devil Wears Prada* (2006) and *Julie and Julia* (2009). He co-wrote, co-directed and starred in *Big Night* (1996) and has directed three other films. In 2012 he published *The Tucci Cookbook*.

The Book Burnings

BERTOLT BRECHT (1898–1956)

→ ←

JACK MAPANJE

This may sound unusual but every time I read this poem, I cry with laughter. Do not ask me why.

The Book Burnings
When the regime ordered that books with harmful knowledge
Should be publicly burnt, and all around
Oxen were forced to drag cartloads of books
To the pyre, one banished poet
One of the best, discovered, studying the list of the burnt
To his horror, that his books
Had been forgotten. He hurried to his desk
On wings of rage and wrote a letter to the powers that be.
Burn me! he wrote, his pen flying, burn me!
Don't do this to me! Don't pass me over! Have I not always told
The truth in my books? And now
I am treated by you as a liar!
                    I order you:
Burn me!

(c. 1941)

TRANSLATION BY TOM KUHN

→ ←

Born in Malawi, Jack Mapanje (b. 1944) is a poet and writer. Head of English at the University of Malawi before being jailed without charge in 1987 – apparently for his collection *Of Chameleons and Gods*, which was seen as critical of President Hastings Banda – he was declared a Prisoner of Conscience by Amnesty International. The many international protests against his imprisonment included a reading of his poems outside the Malawian High Commission in London by Harold Pinter. Released in 1991, he emigrated to the UK, where he wrote a memoir of his experience, *And Crocodiles Are Hungry at Night* (2011), which later became a play. He has since taught English at York, Leeds and Newcastle universities, and creative writing in UK prisons.

Liberté

PAUL ÉLUARD (1895–1952)

➔ ⬅

JOE WRIGHT

I first came across this poem in my late teens and was told by I-can't-remember-who that during the Second World War the RAF dropped thousands of copies of it over occupied France. This legend illustrates for me the social and spiritual power of poetry. In the face of such terror, the delicacy and beauty of hope makes me cry.

Liberty
On my notebooks from school
On my desk and the trees
On the sand on the snow
I write your name

On every page read
On all the white sheets
Stone blood paper or ash
I write your name

On the golden images
On the soldier's weapons

On the crowns of kings
I write your name

On the jungle the desert
The nests and the bushes
On the echo of childhood
I write your name

On the wonder of nights
On the white bread of days
On the seasons engaged
I write your name

On all my blue rags
On the pond mildewed sun
On the lake living moon
I write your name

On the fields the horizon
The wings of the birds
On the windmill of shadows
I write your name

On the foam of the clouds
On the sweat of the storm
On dark insipid rain
I write your name

On the glittering forms
On the bells of colour

On physical truth
I write your name

On the wakened paths
On the opened ways
On the scattered places
I write your name

On the lamp that gives light
On the lamp that is drowned
On my house reunited
I write your name

On the bisected fruit
Of my mirror and room
On my bed's empty shell
I write your name

On my dog greedy tender
On his listening ears
On his awkward paws
I write your name

On the sill of my door
On familiar things
On the fire's sacred stream
I write your name

On all flesh that's in tune
On the brows of my friends

On each hand that extends
I write your name

On the glass of surprises
On lips that attend
High over the silence
I write your name

On my ravaged refuges
On my fallen lighthouses
On the walls of my boredom
I write your name

On passionless absence
On naked solitude
On the marches of death
I write your name

On health that's regained
On danger that's past
On hope without memories
I write your name

By the power of the word
I regain my life
I was born to know you
And to name you
LIBERTY

(1942)

TRANSLATION BY A. S. KLINE

The films directed by Joe Wright (b. 1972) include *Pride and Prejudice* (2005), *Atonement* (2007), *The Soloist* (2009), *Hanna* (2011), *Anna Karenina* (2012) and *Pan* (2015). He has also directed the television miniseries *The Last King* (2003) and London theatre productions of *Trelawny of the Wells* and *A Season in the Congo* (both 2013).

Extract from *The Pisan Cantos*

EZRA POUND (1885–1972)

➔ ⬑

CRAIG RAINE

These passages are taken from the beginning and the end of *The Pisan Cantos*, a poem impossible to divorce from the circumstances of its composition. It is a poem written out of crushing defeat, the defeat of Mussolini, whom Ezra Pound supported.

Like Raleigh in the Tower, Pound wrote in prison, a US detention centre – actually a cage, open to the elements, just outside Pisa. There he typed this great affirmation to the human spirit – telling us what we cling to in extremis ('a lizard upheld me'), lamenting the vanity of human endeavour, affirming the importance of love, seeing noble intention pulsing still in the ashes of defeat.

From 'Canto LXXXI' from *The Pisan Cantos*:
What thou lovest well remains,

                    the rest is dross
What thou lov'st well shall not be reft from thee
What thou lov'st well is thy true heritage
Whose world, or mine or theirs

                or is it of none?

First came the seen, then thus the palpable
    Elysium, though it were in the halls of hell,
What thou lovest well is thy true heritage
What thou lov'st well shall not be reft from thee

The ant's a centaur in his dragon world.
Pull down thy vanity, it is not man
Made courage, or made order, or made grace,
    Pull down thy vanity, I say pull down.
Learn of the green world what can be thy place
In scaled invention or true artistry,
Pull down thy vanity,
                 Paquin pull down!
The green casque has outdone your elegance.

'Master thyself, then others shall thee beare'
    Pull down thy vanity
Thou art a beaten dog beneath the hail,
A swollen magpie in a fitful sun,
Half black, half white
Nor knowst'ou wing from tail
Pull down thy vanity
        How mean thy hates
Fostered in falsity,
        Pull down thy vanity,
Rathe to destroy, niggard in charity,
Pull down thy vanity,
      I say pull down.

But to have done instead of not doing
      this is not vanity

To have, with decency, knocked
That a Blunt should open
         To have gathered from the air a live tradition
or from a fine old eye the unconquered flame
This is not vanity
      Here error is all in the not done,
all in the diffidence that faltered . . .

And I love two lines, rescued from Chaucer, just before this:

'Your eyen two wol sleye me sodenly
I may the beauté of hem nat susteyne.'

From 'Canto LXXIV':
. . . and there was a smell of mint under the tent flaps
especially after the rain
                  and a white ox on the road toward Pisa
                        as if facing the tower,
dark sheep in the drill field and on wet days were clouds
in the mountain as if under the guard roosts.
      A lizard upheld me . . .

                                          (1944–1945)

➔ ◆

Also a critic, librettist and novelist, the poet Craig Raine (b. 1944) is
known for cofounding the 'Martian School' of poetry. For many years
a Fellow at New College, Oxford, he founded and edits the literary
journal *Areté*.

I see a girl dragged by the wrists

PHILIP LARKIN (1922–85)

→ ←

SIMON RUSSELL BEALE

When I first read this poem, the last lines made me gasp with surprise. They also confused me, as I think they are meant to, because the writing suddenly expands and the skies open, promising something almost too weighty for the poet's argument to bear.

Larkin is, of course, the master of charting quotidian disappointments – how small failures can build until they define a life.

All of us, I suspect, have felt what he feels, and some of us have longed for a redemptive, defining experience of the sort that the 'snow-white unicorn' represents. It is this longing that Shakespeare tapped into when he wrote his last plays; and this poem, like those plays, articulates an uncertainty about the significance of that longing. Is hope for redemption, forgiveness, or validation a fantasy? Is resignation to something imperfect or essentially meaningless the only rational option when evaluating one's life? Or is it possible, 'against all argument', as Larkin puts it, that we can believe in the possibility of a fabulous unicorn?

I suppose I hope the latter option is viable, but I am uncertain. That is why the emotional fragility of this poem 'dries my throat'.

I see a girl dragged by the wrists

I see a girl dragged by the wrists
Across a dazzling field of snow,
And there is nothing in me that resists.
Once it would not be so;
Once I should choke with powerless jealousies;
But now I seem devoid of subtlety,
As simple as the things I see,
Being no more, no less, than two weak eyes.

There is snow everywhere,
Snow in one blinding light.
Even snow smudged in her hair
As she laughs and struggles, and pretends to fight;
And still I have no regret;
Nothing so wild, nothing so glad as she
Rears up in me,
And would not, though I watched an hour yet.

So I walk on. Perhaps what I desired
– That long and sickly hope, someday to be
As she is – gave a flicker and expired;
For the first time I'm content to see
What poor mortar and bricks
I have to build with, knowing that I can
Never in seventy years be more a man
Than now – a sack of meal upon two sticks.

So I walk on. And yet the first brick's laid.
Else how should two old ragged men

Clearing the drifts with shovels and a spade
Bring up my mind to fever-pitch again?
How should they sweep the girl clean from my heart,
With no more done
Than to stand coughing in the sun,
Then stoop and shovel snow onto a cart?

The beauty dries my throat.
Now they express
All that's content to wear a worn-out coat,
All actions done in patient hopelessness,
All that ignores the silences of death,
Thinking no further than the hand can hold,
All that grows old,
Yet works on uselessly with shortened breath.

Damn all explanatory rhymes!
To be that girl! – but that's impossible,
For me the task's to learn the many times
When I must stoop, and throw a shovelful:
I must repeat until I live the fact
That everything's remade
With shovel and spade;
That each dull day and each despairing act

Builds up the crags from which the spirit leaps
 – The beast most innocent
That is so fabulous it never sleeps;
If I can keep against all argument
Such image of a snow-white unicorn,

Then as I pray it may for sanctuary
Descend at last to me,
And put into my hand its golden horn.

(1944)

→ ←

As well as playing many of the major Shakespearean roles, most recently King Lear in Sam Mendes's production at London's National Theatre, Simon Russell Beale (b. 1961) has also appeared onstage in roles as varied as Konstantin in Chekhov's *The Seagull* (1991), King Arthur in *Spamalot* (2005), Stalin in *Collaborators* (2011) and Terri Dennis in Peter Nichols's *Privates on Parade* (2013). He has appeared in such films as Kenneth Branagh's *Hamlet* (1996), *The Deep Blue Sea* (2011) and *My Week with Marilyn* (2011), played roles from Schubert to John Adams on television, George Smiley in BBC Radio's adaptation of John le Carré's Smiley novels (2009–10), and danced with the Royal Ballet in *Alice's Adventures in Wonderland* (2011).

The Mother

GWENDOLYN BROOKS (1917–2000)

➤ ⬅

TERRANCE HAYES

The kinds of poems that make a grown man cry are not necessarily the same poems that make a young man cry. Encountering Gwendolyn Brooks's 1945 poem 'The Mother' one lonely afternoon as a college painting major and basketball jock brought abundant tears. It is, in fact, the poem that made me choose the path of a poet rather than that of a painter. (No painting had ever made me cry.) The first word of 'The Mother' tells you some of what a young man could have experienced to be so moved by such a poem. That it continues to move me as an adult is a testament to its craftsmanship. It is the only poem I know, for example, that shifts seamlessly from second-person address in the first stanza to persona poem in the second stanza. The poem begins speaking intimately *to* a mother and ends speaking *as* a mother. I've never tired of 'The Mother'. Maybe the question is: can a poem make a man cry more than once? One always hopes the poem that prompts tears can withstand the sobering, scrutinising gaze of time.

The Mother

Abortions will not let you forget.
You remember the children you got that you did not get,
The damp small pulps with a little or with no hair,
The singers and workers that never handled the air.
You will never neglect or beat
Them, or silence or buy with a sweet.
You will never wind up the sucking-thumb
Or scuttle off ghosts that come.
You will never leave them, controlling your luscious sigh,
Return for a snack of them, with gobbling mother-eye.

I have heard in the voices of the wind the voices of my dim killed
    children.
I have contracted. I have eased
My dim dears at the breasts they could never suck.
I have said, Sweets, if I sinned, if I seized
Your luck
And your lives from your unfinished reach,
If I stole your births and your names,
Your straight baby tears and your games,
Your stilted or lovely loves, your tumults, your marriages, aches,
    and your deaths,
If I poisoned the beginnings of your breaths,
Believe that even in my deliberateness I was not deliberate.
Though why should I whine,
Whine that the crime was other than mine? –
Since anyhow you are dead.
Or rather, or instead,
You were never made.
But that too, I am afraid,

Is faulty: oh, what shall I say, how is the truth to be said?
You were born, you had body, you died.
It is just that you never giggled or planned or cried.

Believe me, I loved you all.
Believe me, I knew you, though faintly, and I loved, I loved you
All.

(1945)

→ ←

Terrance Hayes (b. 1971) won the National Book Award for Poetry with his 2010 collection *Lighthead*. His previous collections are *Muscular Music* (1999), *Hip Logic* (2002) and *Wind in a Box* (2006). His work has appeared in journals from the *Kenyon Review* to the *New Yorker*. He is a Professor of Creative Writing at the University of Pittsburgh.

The Death of
the Ball Turret Gunner

RANDALL JARRELL (1914–65)

➤ ←

PAUL MULDOON

I stopped watching television news reporting in 1991, at precisely the moment we were first shown images purporting to represent 'precision' or 'smart' bombs falling on Iraq, including heavily populated cities such as Baghdad.

My main reason for giving up television news reporting was that the element of reporting was now clearly absent and has remained absent pretty much ever since. More immediately, though, as someone who had lived in Belfast between 1969 and 1986, I had a sense that bombs are neither precise nor smart.

What Randall Jarrell's amazing five-line poem achieves for me is no less than bringing to the front of the mind the horror of modern warfare. Written in 1945, it is a poem in dialogue with Yeats's 'An Irish Airman Foresees His Death' and 'In Memory of Major Robert Gregory', both collected in *The Wild Swans at Coole* (1919). The 'ball turret' in the title of Jarrell's poem is a de-romanticised version of Yeats's signature 'tower set on the stream's edge'. Another poem to which Jarrell alludes is Richard Eberhart's 'The Fury of

Aerial Bombardment', also first published in 1945, with its frank final stanza:

> Of Van Wettering I speak, and Averill,
> Names on a list, whose faces I do not recall
> But they are gone to early death, who late in school
> Distinguished the belt feed lever from the belt holding pawl.

The 'belt feed lever' and the 'belt holding pawl', technical terms which might easily have strayed from Henry Reed's great nuts-and-bolts poem 'Naming of Parts', first published in 1942, are significant components of the machine guns lodged in the Plexiglas dome of the ball turret.

Though I think of this poem often, the thought of the unceremonious hosing from the turret of what's left of the gunner never diminishes in power and never fails to make me weep.

The Death of the Ball Turret Gunner

From my mother's sleep I fell into the State,
And I hunched in its belly till my wet fur froze.
Six miles from earth, loosed from its dream of life,
I woke to black flak and the nightmare fighters.
When I died they washed me out of the turret with a hose.

A ball turret was a Plexiglas sphere set into the belly of a B-17 or B-24, and inhabited by two .50 caliber machine guns and one man, a short small man. When this gunner tracked with his machine guns a fighter attacking his bomber from below, he revolved with the turret; hunched upside-down in his little sphere, he looked like the foetus in the womb. The fighters which attacked him were armed with cannon firing explosive shells. The hose was a steam hose.

– Jarrell's note.

(1945)

➔ ◆

The Irish poet Paul Muldoon (b. 1951) has published more than thirty collections, most recently *The Word on the Street* (2013). A Pulitzer and T. S. Eliot Prize winner, he was Oxford Professor of Poetry from 1999 to 2004. At Princeton University, he is the Howard G. B. Clark '21 Professor in the Humanities and was founding chair of the Lewis Center for the Arts. He is also Poetry Editor of *The New Yorker*.

War Has Been Brought
into Disrepute

BERTOLT BRECHT (1898–1956)

→ ←

DAVID HARE

Reading this poem is like standing at the Cenotaph in London and hearing the first bars of Elgar's 'Nimrod' Variation: it has the same extraordinary visceral power that comes from something complete being said.

I very much admire a saying of Len Deighton's which has the same effect: 'When old men decide to barter young men for pride and profit, the transaction is called war.' All of us who have lived through the last ten years know the relevance of both Brecht's poem and Deighton's observation.

War Has Been Brought into Disrepute
I hear it is being said in respectable circles
That from the moral point of view the Second World War
Did not come up to the First. The *Wehrmacht*
Is said to deplore the means by which the SS
Effected the extermination of certain peoples. In the Ruhr
It seems, the Captains of Industry regret the bloody razzias
That filled their mines and factories with slaves. The intelligentsia

So I hear, condemn the industrialists' demand for such slave
   workers
And their shabby treatment. Even the Bishops
Are distancing themselves from this way of waging war. In short
On all sides there is a feeling that unfortunately
The Nazis have done us a disservice and that war
Of itself a natural and necessary thing, by being conducted
On this occasion in so heedless and indeed inhuman a fashion
Has been, and will be for quite some time
Discredited.

(c. 1945)

TRANSLATION BY DAVID CONSTANTINE

→ ←

The British playwright and director Sir David Hare (b. 1947) has
written some forty plays and TV scripts, among them *Plenty* (1978),
Licking Hitler (1978), *Pravda* (1985, with Howard Brenton), *Strap-
less* (1989), *The Absence of War* (1993), *The Blue Room* (1998)
and *Stuff Happens* (2004). He has also written screenplays for such
films as *The Hours* (2002) and *The Reader* (2008).

Le Message

JACQUES PRÉVERT (1900–77)

→ ←

PETER SÍS

I was born in Czechoslovakia, a country where the door was always closed. You could not go outside, you could just dream about it. Then someone opened the door just a little bit and we could see the ocean and the rainbows. But then the door closed again.

So I was sad, trying to remember what it was that I had seen. I might have even cried. And that was just when I discovered Jacques Prévert's 'Le Message'.

For me it was about the freedom of walking through the door. It was the 1970s and a young man in my country burned himself to death because he believed it.

The Message
The door that someone opened
The door that someone closed
The chair on which someone sat
The cat that someone petted
The fruit that someone bit into
The letter that someone read
The chair that someone tipped over

The door that someone opened
The road that someone ran down
The woods that someone crossed
The river in which someone jumped
The hospital where someone died.

(C. 1950)

TRANSLATION BY TERRY LAJTHA

→ ←

Born in Brno, Moravia, in 1949, Peter Sís today lives and works in New York as an artist, author and filmmaker. A 2003 MacArthur Fellow, he has created award-winning animated shorts and films, tapestries, stage designs and murals. He has written and illustrated numerous books for adults and children, including *Komodo!* (1993), *Starry Messenger: Galileo Galilei* (1996), *Tibet Through the Red Box* (1998), *The Tree of Life: Charles Darwin* (2003) and *The Wall: Growing Up Behind the Iron Curtain* (2007). He received the Hans Christian Andersen Award for his body of work in 2012.

Do Not Go Gentle Into That Good Night

DYLAN THOMAS (1914–53)

→ ←

BENJAMIN ZEPHANIAH

I don't really have a connection to this poem. Thomas wrote it while his father was dying, but I didn't know my father was dying while it was happening, and when I heard that he had died my reaction was minimal. I was actually in my thirties when I discovered this poem, and it touched me on two levels. First, it is a brilliant example of a villanelle, a very difficult poetic form. Dylan Thomas packs so much emotion into it, and not a word is wasted.

But it is not the form that moves me to tears: it's the love I can feel that he has for his father, the desperation in his 'voice' as he is willing his father to live. He is grabbing his father with his words and shaking him, pleading with him not to fade, but to rage. I haven't talked to a therapist about this, but there might also be something here about his having the kind of love for his father that I never had for mine.

Do Not Go Gentle Into That Good Night
Do not go gentle into that good night,
Old age should burn and rave at close of day;
Rage, rage against the dying of the light.

Though wise men at their end know dark is right,
Because their words had forked no lightning they
Do not go gentle into that good night.

Good men, the last wave by, crying how bright
Their frail deeds might have danced in a green bay,
Rage, rage against the dying of the light.

Wild men who caught and sang the sun in flight,
And learn, too late, they grieved it on its way,
Do not go gentle into that good night.

Grave men, near death, who see with blinding sight
Blind eyes could blaze like meteors and be gay,
Rage, rage against the dying of the light.

And you, my father, there on that sad height,
Curse, bless, me now with your fierce tears, I pray.
Do not go gentle into that good night.
Rage, rage against the dying of the light.

(1951)

→ ←

The writer, dub poet and musician Benjamin Zephaniah (b. 1958) has published four novels, five children's books and seven plays, as well as fourteen volumes of verse, notably *The Dread Affair: Collected Poems* (1985), *Rasta Time in Palestine* (1990) and *Too Black, Too Strong* (2001). His discography includes four singles and six albums, including the first recording made by the Wailers following the death of Bob Marley.

Unfinished Poem

PHILIP LARKIN (1922–85)

→ ←

FRANK KERMODE

Frank Kermode's role in the genesis of this book is detailed in its preface. Although himself the victim of a backhanded public compliment from Larkin –

> If I could talk, I'd be a worthless prof,
> Every other year off,
> Just a jetset egghead, TLS toff,
> Not old toad: Frank Kermode.

– he remained an ardent admirer, describing Larkin in *An Appetite for Poetry* (1989) as 'a poet of extraordinary powers', lamenting that Larkin was 'so echt English that Americans tend to find him dull and insular'. Kermode asked for this poem to be read at his funeral.

Unfinished Poem
I squeezed up the last stair to the room in the roof
And lay on the bed there with my jacket off.
Seeds of light were sown on the failure of evening.
The dew came down. I lay in the quiet, smoking.

That was a way to live – newspaper for sheets,
A candle and spirit stove, and a trouble of shouts
From below somewhere, a town smudgy with traffic!
That was a place to go, that emaciate attic!

For (as you will guess) it was death I had in mind,
Who covets our breath, who seeks and will always find;
To keep out of his thoughts was my whole care,
Yet down among sunlit courts, yes, he was there,

Taking his rents; yes, I had only to look
To see the shape of his head and the shine of his book,
And the creep of the world under his sparrow-trap sky,
To know how little slips his immortal memory.

So it was stale time then, day in, day out,
Blue fug in the room, nothing to do but wait
The start of his feet on the stair, that sad sound
Climbing to cut me from his restless mind

With a sign that the air should stick in my nose like bread,
The light swell up and turn black – so I shammed dead,
Still as a stuck pig, hoping he'd keep concerned
With boys who were making the fig when his back was turned;

And the sun and the stove and the mice and the gnawed paper
Made up the days and nights when I missed supper,
Paring my nails, looking over the farbelow street
Of tramways and bells. But one night I heard the feet.

Step after step they mounted with confidence.
Time shrank. They paused at the top. There was no defence.
I sprawled to my knees. Now they came straight at my door.
This, then, the famous eclipse? The crack in the floor

Widening for one long plunge? In a sharp trice,
The world, lifted and wrung, dripped with remorse.
The fact of breathing tightened into a shroud.
Light cringed. The door swung inwards. Over the threshold

Nothing like death stepped, nothing like death paused,
Nothing like death has such hair, arms so raised.
Why are your feet bare? Was not death to come?
Why is he not here? What summer have you broken from?

(1951)

→ ←

Sir Frank Kermode (1919–2010) was regarded as the foremost literary critic of his generation, the author of such books as *Romantic Image* (1957), *The Sense of an Ending* (1967) and *Shakespeare's Language* (2000). He was Lord Northcliffe Professor of Modern English Literature at University College, London, and the King Edward VII Professor of English Literature at Cambridge University. He also inspired the founding of the *London Review of Books* in 1979.

Over 2,000 Illustrations and a Complete Concordance

ELIZABETH BISHOP (1911–79)

→ ←

JOHN ASHBERY

This poem has always struck me as a wonder. I read it first when I was twenty, in *Partisan Review*, and was moved to write Elizabeth Bishop a fan letter – the only time I've ever done so. I was thrilled to get a postcard from her in return, a view of the Maine coast I think, where she might have been staying that summer. Even though I was barely an adult, the poem seemed to sum up life ahead in its first line 'Thus should have been our travels', and life as viewed in retrospect in the last line, 'and looked and looked our infant sight away', a line which still elicits a vagrant tear after all these years.

Over 2,000 Illustrations and a Complete Concordance
Thus should have been our travels:
serious, engravable.
The Seven Wonders of the World are tired
and a touch familiar, but the other scenes,
innumerable, though equally sad and still,
are foreign. Often the squatting Arab,
or group of Arabs, plotting, probably,

against our Christian Empire,
while one apart, with outstretched arm and hand
points to the Tomb, the Pit, the Sepulcher.
The branches of the date-palms look like files.
The cobbled courtyard, where the Well is dry,
is like a diagram, the brickwork conduits
are vast and obvious, the human figure
far gone in history or theology,
gone with its camel or its faithful horse.
Always the silence, the gesture, the specks of birds
suspended on invisible threads above the Site,
or the smoke rising solemnly, pulled by threads.
Granted a page alone or a page made up
of several scenes arranged in cattycornered rectangles
or circles set on stippled gray,
granted a grim lunette,
caught in the toils of an initial letter,
when dwelt upon, they all resolve themselves.
The eye drops, weighted, through the lines
the burin made, the lines that move apart
like ripples above sand,
dispersing storms, God's spreading fingerprint,
and painfully, finally, that ignite
in watery prismatic white-and-blue.

Entering the Narrows at St. Johns
the touching bleat of goats reached to the ship.
We glimpsed them, reddish, leaping up the cliffs
among the fog-soaked weeds and butter-and-eggs.
And at St. Peter's the wind blew and the sun shone madly.
Rapidly, purposefully, the Collegians marched in lines,

crisscrossing the great square with black, like ants.
In Mexico the dead man lay
in a blue arcade; the dead volcanoes
glistened like Easter lilies.
The jukebox went on playing 'Ay, Jalisco!'
And at Volubilis there were beautiful poppies
splitting the mosaics; the fat old guide made eyes.
In Dingle harbor a golden length of evening
the rotting hulks held up their dripping plush.
The Englishwoman poured tea, informing us
that the Duchess was going to have a baby.
And in the brothels of Marrakesh
the little pockmarked prostitutes
balanced their tea-trays on their heads
and did their belly-dances; flung themselves
naked and giggling against our knees,
asking for cigarettes. It was somewhere near there
I saw what frightened me most of all:
A holy grave, not looking particularly holy,
one of a group under a keyhole-arched stone baldaquin
open to every wind from the pink desert.
An open, gritty, marble trough, carved solid
with exhortation, yellowed
as scattered cattle-teeth;
half-filled with dust, not even the dust
of the poor prophet paynim who once lay there.
In a smart burnoose Khadour looked on amused.

Everything only connected by 'and' and 'and.'
Open the book. (The gilt rubs off the edges
of the pages and pollinates the fingertips.)

Over 2,000 Illustrations and a Complete Concordance   157

Open the heavy book. Why couldn't we have seen
this old Nativity while we were at it?
 – the dark ajar, the rocks breaking with light,
an undisturbed, unbreathing flame,
colorless, sparkless, freely fed on straw,
and, lulled within, a family of pets,
 – and looked and looked our infant sight away.

(1955)

> <

John Ashbery (b. 1927) is the author of more than twenty books of po-
etry, most recently *Quick Question* (2012). Other collections include
Notes from the Air: Selected Later Poems (2007), which was awarded
the International Griffin Poetry Prize, and *Self-Portrait in a Convex
Mirror* (1975), which won the three major American prizes – the Pu-
litzer, the National Book Award, and the National Book Critics Circle
Award. The Library of America published the first volume of his col-
lected poems in 2008, and in 2012 President Obama presented him
with a National Humanities Medal.

End of Summer

STANLEY KUNITZ (1905–2006)

→ ←

NICHOLSON BAKER

Stanley Kunitz was a lonely, kind man, a conscientious objector during World War II who wrote a famous line: 'The night nailed like an orange to my brow'. It's from a poem about his father, who killed himself by drinking poison shortly before Kunitz was born. Long ago I bought a collection of Kunitz's poems and read it on lunch hours, and that's how I discovered a short lyric called 'End of Summer'. I've been muttering it to myself ever since.

When we say that a poem makes us cry, what do we really mean? Sometimes we mean that it makes us cry out inwardly in shocked agreement. That's what happened to me when I read Kunitz saying, as he stood in a field of stubble – he owned a farm in Connecticut – that the year was going to 'turn on its hinge', like a framed poster in a swivelling poster display. And then it happened again when, in the third stanza, looking up, he says that blue 'poured into summer blue'. Who knew that an empty afternoon sky could be so full, so generous, so pourably fluid? But it is. And a hawk is up there, having ridden a spiralling thermal up to the top of an invisible aerial tower.

But now, look – the hawk is breaking away. There's a sudden flash of reflected light from the silo's metal roof, and our poet, rhyming the line with 'tower', realises what's happening to him: 'Part of my life was over.'

That's it. You see? There's this one last moment, the superb moment of sunlit stasis. Everything is in balance, and pure, and almost happy – a moment of en-passant perfection. But it's also the end, because 'already' the iron door of the north is opening. The change isn't imminent, it's already in progress – there's nothing we can do. And finally we come to the last three slow, fatal, resigned syllables: a 'cruel wind blows'.

This poem itself is an orange. Nail it to your brow.

End of Summer
An agitation of the air,
A perturbation of the light
Admonished me the unloved year
Would turn on its hinge that night.

I stood in the disenchanted field
Amid the stubble and the stones,
Amazed, while a small worm lisped to me
The song of my marrow-bones.

Blue poured into summer blue,
A hawk broke from his cloudless tower,
The roof of the silo blazed, and I knew
That part of my life was over.

Already the iron door of the north
Clangs open: birds, leaves, snows
Order their populations forth,
And a cruel wind blows.

(1953)

➜ ⬅

The novels of Nicholson Baker (b. 1957) include *The Mezzanine* (1988), *Vox* (1992), *The Fermata* (1994), and two books narrated by a poet, *The Anthologist* (2009) and *Traveling Sprinkler* (2013). Among his nonfiction works are *U and I* (1991), *Double Fold* (2001) and *Human Smoke* (2008).

The Horses

EDWIN MUIR (1887–1959)

➤ ⬅

ALEXEI SAYLE

First of all, there is a vivid but subtle evocation of some human-made apocalypse; the images of the warship piled with dead and the plane crashing into the sea are haunting and, though used since in lesser works, remain fresh, original and profoundly disturbing. Then there is the suggestion of redemption via a new and respectful relationship with animals and the planet; a new beginning away from the mechanistic ways that brought us to disaster.

All the lines move me, but it's the final two that really get me: 'But that free servitude still can pierce our hearts. / Our life is changed; their coming our beginning.'

The Horses
Barely a twelvemonth after
The seven days war that put the world to sleep,
Late in the evening the strange horses came.
By then we had made our covenant with silence,
But in the first few days it was so still
We listened to our breathing and were afraid.
On the second day

The radios failed; we turned the knobs; no answer.
On the third day a warship passed us, heading north,
Dead bodies piled on the deck. On the sixth day
A plane plunged over us into the sea. Thereafter
Nothing. The radios dumb;
And still they stand in corners of our kitchens,
And stand, perhaps, turned on, in a million rooms
All over the world. But now if they should speak,
If on a sudden they should speak again,
If on the stroke of noon a voice should speak,
We would not listen, we would not let it bring
That old bad world that swallowed its children quick
At one great gulp. We would not have it again.
Sometimes we think of the nations lying asleep,
Curled blindly in impenetrable sorrow,
And then the thought confounds us with its strangeness.
The tractors lie about our fields; at evening
They look like dank sea-monsters couched and waiting.
We leave them where they are and let them rust:
'They'll molder away and be like other loam.'
We make our oxen drag our rusty plows,
Long laid aside. We have gone back
Far past our fathers' land.
    And then, that evening
Late in the summer the strange horses came.
We heard a distant tapping on the road,
A deepening drumming; it stopped, went on again
And at the corner changed to hollow thunder.
We saw the heads
Like a wild wave charging and were afraid.
We had sold our horses in our fathers' time

To buy new tractors. Now they were strange to us
As fabulous steeds set on an ancient shield
Or illustrations in a book of knights.
We did not dare go near them. Yet they waited,
Stubborn and shy, as if they had been sent
By an old command to find our whereabouts
And that long-lost archaic companionship.
In the first moment we had never a thought
That they were creatures to be owned and used.
Among them were some half-a-dozen colts
Dropped in some wilderness of the broken world,
Yet new as if they had come from their own Eden.
Since then they have pulled our plows and borne our loads
But that free servitude still can pierce our hearts.
Our life is changed; their coming our beginning.

(1956)

→ ←

The writer, actor and comedian Alexei Sayle (b. 1952) has appeared in TV series such as *The Young Ones* and *The Comic Strip Presents . . .* and films such as *Gorky Park* (1983), *Indiana Jones and the Last Crusade* (1989) and *The Thief Lord* (2006). His books include the memoir *Stalin Ate My Homework* (2010).

Friday's Child

W. H. AUDEN (1907–1973)

➤ ◄

ROWAN WILLIAMS

The story of Dietrich Bonhoeffer (1906–45) is moving enough in its own right – the tale of someone who abandoned the chance of safety in order to work for the overthrow of Hitler and paid with his life. But Auden broadens out to see that life as a test case for faith. The poem puts side by side all the intellectual uncertainties around faith, all the reasons for shrugging your shoulders about it and moving on, and then concludes – with a devastating shift of gear – simply by pointing to the figure of the crucified Jesus, silent but changing everything, a God whose apparent 'absence' leaves us free. Like Bonhoeffer's sacrifice and death, this is what actually keeps faith alive, not any ideas or proofs.

Friday's Child

In memory of Dietrich Bonhoeffer,
martyred at Flossenbürg,
9 April 1945

He told us we were free to choose
But, children as we were, we thought –
'Paternal Love will only use
Force in the last resort

On those too bumptious to repent.'
Accustomed to religious dread,
It never crossed our minds He meant
Exactly what He said.

Perhaps He frowns, perhaps He grieves,
But it seems idle to discuss
If anger or compassion leaves
The bigger bangs to us.

What reverence is rightly paid
To a Divinity so odd
He lets the Adam whom He made
Perform the Acts of God?

It might be jolly if we felt
Awe at this Universal Man
(When kings were local, people knelt);
Some try to, but who can?

The self-observed observing Mind
We meet when we observe at all
Is not alarming or unkind
But utterly banal.

Though instruments at Its command
Make wish and counterwish come true,
It clearly cannot understand
What It can clearly do.

Since the analogies are rot
Our senses based belief upon,
We have no means of learning what
Is really going on,

And must put up with having learned
All proofs or disproofs that we tender
Of His existence are returned
Unopened to the sender.

Now, did He really break the seal
And rise again? We dare not say;
But conscious unbelievers feel
Quite sure of Judgement Day.

Meanwhile, a silence on the cross,
As dead as we shall ever be,
Speaks of some total gain or loss,
And you and I are free

To guess from the insulted face
Just what Appearances He saves
By suffering in a public place
A death reserved for slaves.

(1958)

→ ←

A published poet himself, as well as the author of numerous volumes of theology, Rowan Williams (b. 1950) was the 104th Archbishop of Canterbury before he stepped down at the end of 2012. He was made a life peer in 2013 and is now Master of Magdalene College, Cambridge.

Long Distance I and II

TONY HARRISON (1937–)

→ ←

DANIEL RADCLIFFE

Tony Harrison is, in my opinion, the most important English poet of the latter half of the twentieth century. His poems are often brutal and confrontational, but in 'Long Distance I and II' he is simply a son mourning the loss of his parents. If the last line doesn't bring you up short, you have a heart the size of a snow pea!

Long Distance I

Your bed's got two wrong sides. You life's all grouse.
I let your phone-call take its dismal course:

Ah can't stand it no more, this empty house!

Carrots choke us wi'out your mam's white sauce!

Them sweets you brought me, you can have 'em back.
Ah'm diabetic now. Got all the facts.
(The diabetes comes hard on the track
of two coronaries and cataracts.)

Ah've allus liked things sweet! But now ah push
food down mi throat! Ah'd sooner do wi'out.
And t'only reason now for beer 's to flush
(so t'dietician said) mi kidneys out.

When I come round, they'll be laid out, the sweets,
Lifesavers, my father's New World treats,
still in the big brown bag, and only bought
rushing through JFK as a last thought.

Long Distance II
Though my mother was already two years dead
Dad kept her slippers warming by the gas,
put hot water bottles her side of the bed
and still went to renew her transport pass.

You couldn't just drop in. You had to phone.
He'd put you off an hour to give him time
to clear away her things and look alone
as though his still raw love were such a crime.

He couldn't risk my blight of disbelief
though sure that very soon he'd hear her key
scrape in the rusted lock and end his grief.
He knew she'd just popped out to get the tea.

I believe life ends with death, and that is all.
You haven't both gone shopping; just the same,
in my new black leather phone book there's your name
and the disconnected number I still call.

(1960s)

Since playing the title role in all eight Harry Potter films, Daniel Radcliffe (b. 1989) has starred in *The Woman in Black* (2012); *Kill Your Darlings* (2013), in which he played the poet Allen Ginsberg; Alexandre Aja's *Horns* (2014), based on Joe Hill's bestselling book; the romantic comedy *The F Word* and the title role in *Igor* (2015). His theatre credits in London and New York include *Equus* (2007–8), *How to Succeed in Business Without Really Trying* (2011) and *The Cripple of Inishmaan* (2013). His television work includes *David Copperfield* (1999), *Extras* (2006), *My Boy Jack* (2007), and *A Young Doctor's Notebook* (2012). He will next star in the role of Igor in *Frankenstein*.

The Widower in the Country

LES MURRAY (1938–)

→ ←

NICK CAVE

This very sad poem of loss revolves mournfully around the unmentioned death of the farmer's wife, as we follow him through his dire and ineffectual day's work. He is that tough old Australian country man, so familiar to me, just getting on with the business of life – and this is sad enough in itself – but it is the violence of the last two lines, that screaming unconsciousness, that really brings on the waterworks.

The Widower in the Country
I'll get up soon, and leave my bed unmade.
I'll go outside and split off kindling wood,
From the yellow-box log that lies beside the gate,
And the sun will be high, for I get up late now.
I'll drive my axe in the log and come back in
With my armful of wood, and pause to look across
The Christmas paddocks aching in the heat,
The windless trees, the nettles in the yard . . .
And then I'll go in, boil water and make tea.

This afternoon, I'll stand out on the hill
And watch my house away below, and how
The roof reflects the sun and makes my eyes
Water and close on bright webbed visions smeared
On the dark of my thoughts to dance and fade away,
Then the sun will move on, and I will simply watch,
Or work, or sleep. And evening will draw in.

Coming on dark, I'll go home, light the lamp
And eat my corned-beef supper, sitting there
At the head of the table. Then I'll go to bed.
Last night I thought I dreamt – but when I woke
The screaming was only a possum ski-ing down
The iron roof on little moonlit claws.

(1963)

→ ←

Nick Cave (b. 1957) is an Australian musician, composer and writer. He is perhaps best known for being the front man of the band Nick Cave and the Bad Seeds, established in 1983. Cave's other groups include the Birthday Party and Grinderman. He is also the author of novels including *The Death of Bunny Munro* (2009) and the screenwriter of films such as *The Proposition* (2005) and *Lawless* (2012).

A Blessing

JAMES ARLINGTON WRIGHT (1927–80)

→ ←

RICHARD FORD

Accounting for this poem's large effects (its exaction of a tear) reminds me of Johnson's directive about light: it's easy to *know* what light is, but hard (yet sometimes thrilling) to *tell* what it is. In Wright's lovely poem (I heard him read it forty years ago, in Ann Arbor), the thrill seems to come from two sources: the splurge at the end, of course; the freshet of sensation-put-to-words, an appreciative perception that one modest thing can actually cause a much grander one (art's little secret). The other source is the textured evocation of the modest thing itself: the homely narrative of the ponies, the restrained, delicate but strangely alerting imagery attendant ('shyly as wet swans', 'the skin over a girl's wrist'). Add loneliness versus happiness – the big-ticket issues – to the mix. And suddenly something's brewing. We sense it: a commotion of colliding effects – restrained but impending, and seeking an outcome. In imagining that thrilling outcome – 'I would break / Into blossom' – the poem doesn't so much reconcile its commotion as much as treat it as being no longer quite bearable, and so leaps on and through – breathtakingly, if you're me – into pure light.

A Blessing

Just off the highway to Rochester, Minnesota,
Twilight bounds softly forth on the grass.
And the eyes of those two Indian ponies
Darken with kindness.
They have come gladly out of the willows
To welcome my friend and me.
We step over the barbed wire into the pasture
Where they have been grazing all day, alone.
They ripple tensely, they can hardly contain their happiness
That we have come.
They bow shyly as wet swans. They love each other.
There is no loneliness like theirs.
At home once more,
They begin munching the young tufts of spring in the darkness.
I would like to hold the slenderer one in my arms,
For she has walked over to me
And nuzzled my left hand.
She is black and white,
Her mane falls wild on her forehead,
And the light breeze moves me to caress her long ear
That is delicate as the skin over a girl's wrist.
Suddenly I realize
That if I stepped out of my body I would break
Into blossom.

(1963)

→ ←

The novels of Richard Ford (b. 1944) include *The Sportswriter* (1986), *Independence Day* (Pulitzer Prize, 1995), *The Lay of the Land* (2006) and *Canada* (2012). He has also published five volumes of short stories and a screenplay, *Bright Angel* (1990). He is Professor of Writing at the Columbia University School of the Arts in New York.

Injustice

PABLO NERUDA (1904-1973)

→ ←

CARLOS REYES-MANZO

Pablo Neruda raises the veil covering the invisible people in history, the people who are 'disappeared' through poverty and hunger and the 'disappeared' in secret prisons by governments around the world. This poem speaks to me because it encapsulates how people suffer today, and reminds me of the people I meet when I document the inequalities enforced by an unjust economic system.

> And then I stopped being a child
> because I understood that
> they did not allow my people to live
> and they denied them burial.

The last line moves me because I can see what happened in Chile in the past still happens today globally. It is painful to come face to face with people suffering social exclusion. Nothing can justify an unfair economic system that does not allow people to live in peace and justice.

Pablo Neruda's 'Injustice' is a critique addressed to a society that sees poverty and social discrimination from a charity viewpoint, and reminds us that we are judged by our sense of social justice. The poem is a salute to poor people who live with dignity regardless of whether they have a home to live in or a burial place.

Injustice

Whoever discovers who I am will discover who you are.
And the why, and the where.
Suddenly I touched all injustice.
Hunger was not just hunger,
but the measure of humanity.
The cold, the wind, were also measures.
The proud man suffered a hundred hungers and fell.
Pedro was buried after a hundred winters.
The poor house survived only one storm.
And I learned that the centimeter and gram,
the spoon and tongue measured greed,
and that the besieged man falls suddenly
in a hole, and then knows nothing more.
Nothing more, and this was the place,
the real present, the gift, the light, life,
that is what it was, to suffer cold and hunger,
and not to have shoes and to tremble
in front of the judge, in front of another,
the other being with sword or inkwell,
and in this way struggling, digging and cutting,
sewing, making bread, sowing wheat,
hitting every nail that asked for wood,
entering the earth as if in an intestine
to extract, blindly, the crackling coal
and, still more, going up rivers and mountains,
riding horses, pushing out boats,

cooking tiles, blowing glass, washing clothes,

in such a way that it would seem

all this kingdom had just been created,

dazzling grapes from the vine,

when humanity decided to be happy,

and was not, it was not like that. Little by little I discovered

the law of unhappiness,

the throne of bloodied gold,

complicit freedom,

the unprotected motherland,

the wounded and exhausted heart,

and the sound of the dead without tears,

dry, like stones that fall.

And then I stopped being a child

because I understood that

they did not allow my people to live

and they denied them burial.

(1964)

TRANSLATION BY VALERIA BAKER

→ ←

Following the 1973 coup which brought General Pinochet to power, the Chilean photographer and poet Carlos Reyes-Manzo (b. 1944) was imprisoned for two years, then exiled to Panama. Kidnapped by the secret police in 1979, to be sent back to Chile, he escaped from the plane and claimed asylum in London, where he has since lived. His work all over the world documenting conflicts and their victims has resulted in four books and numerous exhibitions. In 2011 Amnesty International, to mark its fiftieth anniversary, appointed him its inaugural poet-in-residence.

The Meaning of Africa

ABIOSEH NICOL (1924–94)

➔ ✦

JAMES EARL JONES

I was rehearsing Lorraine Hansberry's last (but unfinished) play *Les Blancs* for its Broadway premiere – her artistic answer to Jean Genet's caustic 'clown show' about colonialism, called *The Blacks* (*Les Negres*) – and was in need of a point of view for Lorraine's character. He was an African in search of his soul. He had searched in the sophisticated circles of London; now he has returned home to Africa at a chaotic time of liberation. I found Nicol's poem pertinent not only for my character but for myself. The poem confirmed for me that the goal in all life is not necessarily happiness or success, but simply contentment. Nicol's liberation is not of the political sort, but more the psychological. I have found that the plea 'It is only because I have wanted so much / That I have always been found wanting' applies to most of the characters I have ever tried to bring to life on stage.

The Meaning of Africa

Africa, you were once just a name to me
But now you lie before me with sombre green challenge
To that loud faith for freedom (life more abundant)

Which we once professed shouting
Into the silent listening microphone
Or on an alien platform to a sea
Of white perplexed faces troubled
With secret Imperial guilt; shouting
Of you with a vision euphemistic
As you always appear
To your lonely sons on distant shores.

Then the cold sky and continent would disappear
In a grey mental mist.
And in its stead the hibiscus blooms in shameless scarlet
and the bougainvillea in mauve passion
entwines itself around strong branches
the palm trees stand like tall proud moral women
shaking their plaited locks against the
cool suggestive evening breeze;
the short twilight passes;
the white full moon turns its round gladness
towards the swept open space
between the trees; there will be
dancing tonight; and in my brimming heart
plenty of love and laughter.
Oh, I got tired of the cold northern sun
Of white anxious ghost-like faces
Of crouching over heatless fires
In my lonely bedroom.
The only thing I never tired of
was the persistent kindness
Of you too few unafraid
Of my grave dusky strangeness.

So I came back
Sailing down the Guinea Coast.
Loving the sophistication
Of your brave new cities:
Dakar, Accra, Cotonou,
Lagos, Bathurst and Bissau;
Liberia, Freetown, Libreville,
Freedom is really in the mind.

Go up-country, so they said,
To see the real Africa.
For whomsoever you may be,
That is where you come from.
Go for bush, inside the bush,
You will find your hidden heart,
Your mute ancestral spirit.
So I went, dancing on my way.

Now you lie before me passive
With your unanswering green challenge.
Is this all you are?
This long uneven red road, this occasional succession
Of huddled heaps of four mud walls
And thatched, falling grass roofs
Sometimes ennobled by a thin layer
Of white plaster, and covered with thin
Slanting corrugated zinc.
These patient faces on weather-beaten bodies
Bowing under heavy market loads.
The pedalling cyclist wavers by

On the wrong side of the road,
As if uncertain of his new emancipation.
The squawking chickens, the pregnant she-goats
Lumber awkwardly with fear across the road,
Across the windscreen view of my four-cylinder kit car.
An overloaded lorry speeds madly towards me
Full of produce, passengers, with driver leaning
Out into the swirling dust to pilot his
Swinging obsessed vehicle along,
Beside him on the raised seat his first-class
Passenger, clutching and timid; but he drives on
At so, so many miles per hour, peering out with
Bloodshot eyes, unshaved face and dedicated look;
His motto painted on each side: Sunshine Transport,
We get you there quick, quick. The Lord is my Shepherd.

The red dust settles down on the green leaves.

I know you will not make me want, Lord,
Though I have reddened your green pastures
It is only because I have wanted so much
That I have always been found wanting.
From South and East, and from my West
(The sandy desert holds the North)
We look across a vast continent
And blindly call it ours.

You are not a country, Africa,
You are a concept,
Fashioned in our minds, each to each,
To hide our separate fears,

To dream our separate dreams.
Only those within you who know
Their circumscribed plot,
And till it well with steady plough
Can from that harvest then look up
To the vast blue inside
Of the enamelled bowl of sky
Which covers you and say
'This is my Africa' meaning
'I am content and happy.
I am fulfilled, within,
Without and roundabout
I have gained the little longings
Of my hands, my loins, my heart
And the soul that follows in my shadow.'
I know now that is what you are, Africa:
Happiness, contentment, and fulfilment,
And a small bird singing on a mango tree.

(1964)

→ ←

James Earl Jones (b. 1931) made his Broadway debut in 1957 and has since played many Shakespearean and classical parts from the title roles in *Othello* and *King Lear* to, more recently, *On Golden Pond* (2005), *Cat on a Hot Tin Roof* (2008–9), *Driving Miss Daisy* (2010–11) and *Much Ado About Nothing* (2013). His 100-plus TV and film credits range from *Dr Strangelove* (1964) and *The Great White Hope* (1970) to *Claudine* (1974), *Field of Dreams* (1989), *The Hunt for Red October* (1990), *Cry, the Beloved Country* (1995) and *Gimme Shelter* (2013). He is also the voice of Darth Vader in the *Star Wars* series. His numerous awards include two Tonys, two Emmys and an honorary Academy Award.

Elegy for Alto

CHRISTOPHER OKIGBO (1932-67)

→ ←

BEN OKRI

The poem I have chosen is by Christopher Okigbo. It is from his only volume of poems, *Labyrinths*. In it there is a sequence called *The Path of Thunder: Poem Prophesying War*. And I have chosen 'Elegy for Alto' from that sequence. What moves me about the poem is its solemn beauty, its music, its prophetic roll, which leads on to the poet prophesying his own death. It is impossible to separate what moves me in this poem from the inner nature of the way it is written. The poet seems to have gone beyond the rim of ordinary experience, to have wandered to the outer constellations of what it is to be human.

Okigbo is writing about a time of political and cultural disintegration in Nigeria in the sixties. He freights across these omens of war, signs of disaster. He is writing about the onset of the Nigerian civil war, in which he perished. His death, and the slender but distinguished body of poems he left behind, contribute to his legend. His death is implicated in the poem in advance, as it were; one reads it with tears for the death of the poet as well as for the death of his nation's innocence.

Elegy for Alto
with drum accompaniment

AND THE HORN may now paw the air howling goodbye . . .

For the Eagles are now in sight:
Shadows in the horizon –

THE ROBBERS are here in black sudden steps of showers, of
    caterpillars –

THE EAGLES have come again,
The eagles rain down on us –

POLITICIANS are back in giant hidden steps of howitzers, of
    detonators –

THE EAGLES descend on us,
Bayonets and cannons –

THE ROBBERS descend on us to strip us of our laughter, of our
    thunder –

THE EAGLES have chosen their game,
Taken our concubines –

POLITICIANS are here in this iron dance of mortars, of
    generators –

THE EAGLES are suddenly there,
New stars of iron dawn;

So let the horn paw the air howling goodbye . . .

O mother, mother Earth, unbind me; let this be
  my last testament; let this be
The ram's hidden wish to the sword, the sword's
  secret prayer to the scabbard –

THE ROBBERS are back in black hidden steps of detonators –

FOR BEYOND the blare of sirened afternoons, beyond the
  motorcades;
Beyond the voices and days, the echoing highways; beyond the
  latescence
Of our dissonant airs; through our curtained eyeballs,
  through our shuttered sleep,
Onto our forgotten selves, onto our broken images;
  beyond the barricades
Commandments and edicts, beyond the iron tables,
  beyond the elephant's
Legendary patience, beyond his inviolable bronze
  bust; beyond our crumbling towers –

BEYOND the iron path careering along the same beaten track –

THE GLIMPSE of a dream lies smouldering in a cave,
  together with the mortally wounded birds.
Earth, unbind me; let me be the prodigal; let this be
  the ram's ultimate prayer to the tether . . .

AN OLD STAR departs, leaves us here on the shore
Gazing heavenward for a new star approaching;

The new star appears, foreshadows its going
Before a going and coming that goes on forever . . .

(1965–1967)

➔ ◀

The Nigerian-born, UK-resident writer Ben Okri (b. 1959) won the 1991 Booker Prize for his third novel *The Famished Road*, the first volume of an African trilogy continued in *Songs of Enchantment* (1993) and *Infinite Riches* (1998). His other novels include *Starbook* (2007) and *The Age of Magic* (2014). He and has also published poetry, essays and short stories, including *Tales of Freedom* (2009), *A Time for New Dreams* (2011) and a volume of poems, *Wild* (2012).

Requiem for the Croppies

SEAMUS HEANEY (1939–2013)

→ ←

TERRY GEORGE

The images evoked of the great Irish rebellion of 1798 are poignant and moving. The population – tramp, priest, and peasant – rose up in its thousands against tyrannical British rule. They fought with pikes and farm tools against cannon. The men carried barley seed in their pockets as food on the march, and the following summer, after their inevitable defeat, the barley sprouted from their mass graves. A devastatingly sad image.

Requiem for the Croppies
The pockets of our greatcoats full of barley . . .
No kitchens on the run, no striking camp . . .
We moved quick and sudden in our own country.
The priest lay behind ditches with the tramp.
A people hardly marching . . . on the hike . . .
We found new tactics happening each day:
We'd cut through reins and rider with the pike
And stampede cattle into infantry,
Then retreat through hedges where cavalry must be thrown.
Until . . . on Vinegar Hill . . . the final conclave.

Terraced thousands died, shaking scythes at cannon.
The hillside blushed, soaked in our broken wave.
They buried us without shroud or coffin
And in August . . . the barley grew up out of our grave.

(1966)

→ ←

The Belfast-born screenwriter and director Terry George (b. 1952) is the author of various screenplays, notably *In the Name of the Father* (1993). In 1996 George made his directorial debut with *Some Mother's Son*. Since then he has written and directed numerous television shows and feature films including *A Bright Shining Lie* (1998), *The District* (2000–4), *Hart's War* (2002) and *Reservation Road* (2007). In 2004 he wrote, directed and produced *Hotel Rwanda,* and his latest feature film is *Whole Lotta Sole* (2011). In 2012 George and his daughter, Oorlagh, won the Academy Award for Live Action Short Film for their Northern Ireland reconciliation story *The Shore*.

Gone Ladies

CHRISTOPHER LOGUE (1926–2011)

→ ←

BRIAN PATTEN

Christopher Logue wrote 'Gone Ladies' in 1966 and dedicated it to the artist Pauline Boty, who died that year at the age of twenty-eight. In 1978 her husband, Clive Goodwin, died of a brain haemorrhage in a Los Angeles lockup where he'd been thrown by the police. They thought he was drunk. Boty Goodwin, their daughter, as heart-stoppingly beautiful as her mother, died seventeen years after that, at the age of twenty-nine.

'Gone Ladies' is an adaptation of Villon's *'Ballade des dames du temps jadis'*, written in the twelfth century. It is an elegy for real and mythical women, their beauty, and how it vanishes, like – as Dante Gabriel Rossetti says in an earlier translation – 'the snows of yesteryear'. It also evokes a far broader sadness, the sadness one feels for all gone friends.

Gone Ladies
Where in the world is Helen gone,
Whose loveliness demolished Troy?
Where is Salome?
Where the wan licentious cream of Avalon?
Who sees my lady Fontenoy

And where is Joan, so soldier tall?
And she who bore God's only boy?
Where is the snow we watched last Fall?

Is Thaïs still? Is Nell? And can
Stem Héloïse aurene,
Whose so-by-love-enchanted man
Sooner would risk castration than
Abandon her, be seen?
Who does Scheherazade enthral?
And who, within her arms and small,
Shares Sappho's evergreen?

Through what eventless territory
Are ladies Day and Joplin swept?
What news of Marilyn who crept
Into an endless reverie?
You saw Lucrece? And Jane? And she,
Salvations's ancient blame-it-all,
Delicious Eve? Then answer me:
Where is the snow we watched last Fall?

Girl never see to know from me
Who was the fairest of them all.
What wouldst thou say if I asked thee:
Where is the snow we watched last Fall?

(1966)

→ ←

Brian Patten (b. 1946) made his name in the 1960s as one of the Liv-
erpool Poets, alongside Adrian Henri and Roger McGough with their

joint anthology, *The Mersey Sound* (1967), which is now a Penguin Modern Classic. He has published more than forty books, including *Collected Love Poems* and *Selected Poems* (2007). He writes for both children and adults and his poems are translated into many European languages.

Dream Song 90:
Op. posth. no. 13

JOHN BERRYMAN (1914–72)

→ ←

AL ALVAREZ

John Berryman wrote this poem about his friend Randall Jarrell.

As it happens, Jarrell was not one of the young writers who gathered around Richard Blackmur, though like most of them – Berryman, Delmore Schwartz, Robert Lowell, Theodore Roethke – he died badly and too soon. But, whenever I read Berryman's lines about 'the beloved faces', I think of Blackmur and Princeton, of being young and ambitious and full of ideas and of arguing all night with Kenneth Burke. And sometimes the poem makes me wish that I, too, believed in an afterlife – if only because I know that if I ran into Burke up there we'd go on with the argument, and all would be as before.

Dream Song 90: Op. posth. no. 13
In the night-reaches dreamed he of better graces,
of liberations, and beloved faces,
such as now ere dawn he sings.
It would not be easy, accustomed to these things,
to give up the old world, but he could try;
let it all rest, have a good cry.

Let Randall rest, whom your self-torturing
cannot restore one instant's good to, rest:
he's left us now.
The panic died and in the panic's dying
so did my old friend. I am headed west
also, also, somehow.

In the chambers of the end we'll meet again
I will say Randall, he'll say Pussycat
and all will be as before
whenas we sought, among the beloved faces,
eminence and were dissatisfied with that
and needed more.

(c. 1968)

→ ←

The poet, critic and novelist Al Alvarez (b. 1929) is the author of two
seminal works on twentieth-century poetry, his 1962 anthology *The
New Poetry* and his 1971 study of suicide and literature, *The Savage
God*. He has been a champion of Sylvia Plath, Miroslav Holub and
Zbigniew Herbert, among many other European and American poets.
His choice evokes memories of his time as a young man at Princeton,
as recalled in his 1999 autobiography *Where Did It All Go Right?*

Essay

HAYDEN CARRUTH (1921–2008)

→ ←

JONATHAN FRANZEN

The line that gets me is 'They are going away'.

Essay
So many poems about the deaths of animals.
Wilbur's toad, Kinnell's porcupine, Eberhart's squirrel,
and that poem by someone – Hecht? Merrill? –
about cremating a woodchuck. But mostly
I remember the outrageous number of them,
as if *every* poet, I too, had written at least
one animal elegy; with the result that today
when I came to a good enough poem by Edwin Brock
about finding a dead fox at the edge of the sea
I could not respond; as if permanent shock
had deadened me. And then after a moment
I began to give way to sorrow (watching myself
sorrowlessly the while), not merely because
part of my being had been violated and annulled,
but because all these many poems over the years
have been necessary, – suitable and correct. This

has been the time of the finishing off of the animals.
They are going away – their fur and their wild eyes,
their voices. Deer leap and leap in front
of the screaming snowmobiles until they leap
out of existence. Hawks circle once or twice
around their shattered nests and then they climb
to the stars. I have lived with them fifty years,
we have lived with them fifty million years,
and now they are going, almost gone. I don't know
if the animals are capable of reproach.
But clearly they do not bother to say good-bye.

(1970s)

→ ‹

Jonathan Franzen (b. 1959) is a novelist, essayist, journalist and trans-
lator. His novels include *The Corrections* (2001) and *Freedom* (2010).
His most recent book is *The Kraus Project* (2013).

An Exequy

PETER PORTER (1929–2010)

→ ←

IAN MCEWAN

Peter Porter's wife, Jannice, killed herself in her childhood attic bedroom in 1974. The elegy he wrote some months later is perhaps the finest in modern poetry. It borrows the form of Henry King's seventeenth-century lament for the death of his young wife, 'The Exequy'. With typical modesty, Porter substitutes 'an' for 'the'. His four-beat lines, mostly end-stopped, have a funereal quality, heavy with grief, reminding us of King's famous couplet, 'But hark! my pulse like a soft drum / Beats my approach, tells thee I come'; but where King writes in the conventional expectation of a reconciliation in the afterlife, Porter's poem is troubled by guilt ('Black creatures of the upper deep') and despair – 'The abstract hell of memory / The pointlessness of poetry'. There are moments of wry humour too, recollecting a visit to Venice – 'Doing each masterpiece the kindness / Of discovering it'. But the emotional heart of the elegy comes at the point at which this most scholarly of poets abandons all cultural allusion to acknowledge in simple, tender lines the death he owes his wife –

When your slim shape from photographs
Stands at my door and gently asks

If I have any work to do
Or will I come to bed with you.

Now that Peter too has gone and that deeply troubled marriage is a
faded memory, this evocation of domestic intimacy, which is also a
ghostly beckoning towards death, seems all the more poignant.

An Exequy

In wet May, in the months of change,
In a country you wouldn't visit, strange
Dreams pursue me in my sleep,
Black creatures of the upper deep –
Though you are five months dead, I see
You in guilt's iconography,
Dear Wife, lost beast, beleaguered child,
The stranded monster with the mild
Appearance, whom small waves tease,
(Andromeda upon her knees
In orthodox deliverance)
And you alone of pure substance,
The unformed form of life, the earth
Which Piero's brushes brought to birth
For all to greet as myth, a thing
Out of the box of imagining.

This introduction serves to sing
Your mortal death as Bishop King
Once hymned in tetrametric rhyme
His young wife, lost before her time;
Though he lived on for many years
His poem each day fed new tears

To that unreaching spot, her grave,
His lines a baroque architrave
The Sunday poor with bottled flowers
Would by-pass in their morning hours,
Esteeming ragged natural life
('Most dearly loved, most gentle wife'),
Yet, looking back when at the gate
And seeing grief in formal state
Upon a sculpted angel group,
Were glad that men of god could stoop
To give the dead a public stance
And freeze them in their mortal dance.

The words and faces proper to
My misery are private – you
Would never share your heart with those
Whose only talent's to suppose,
Nor from your final childish bed
Raise a remote confessing head –
The channels of our lives are blocked,
The hand is stopped upon the clock,
No one can say why hearts will break
And marriages are all opaque:
A map of loss, some posted cards,
The living house reduced to shards,
The abstract hell of memory,
The pointlessness of poetry –
These are the instances which tell
Of something which I know full well,
I owe a death to you – one day
The time will come for me to pay

When your slim shape from photographs
Stands at my door and gently asks
If I have any work to do
Or will I come to bed with you.
O scala enigmata,
I'll climb up to that attic where
The curtain of your life was drawn
Some time between despair and dawn –
I'll never know with what halt steps
You mounted to this plain eclipse
But each stair now will station me
A black responsibility
And point me to that shut-down room,
'This be your due appointed tomb.'

I think of us in Italy:
Gin-and-chianti-fuelled, we
Move in a trance through Paradise,
Feeding at last our starving eyes,
Two people of the English blindness
Doing each masterpiece the kindness
Of discovering it – from Baldovinetti
To Venice's most obscure jetty.
A true unfortunate traveller, I
Depend upon your nurse's eye
To pick the altars where no Grinner
Puts us off our tourists' dinner
And in hotels to bandy words
With Genevan girls and talking birds,
To wear your feet out following me
To night's end and true amity,

And call my rational fear of flying
A paradigm of Holy Dying –
And, oh my love, I wish you were
Once more with me, at night somewhere
In narrow streets applauding wines,
The moon above the Apennines
As large as logic and the stars,
Most middle-aged of avatars,
As bright as when they shone for truth
Upon untried and avid youth.

The rooms and days we wandered through
Shrink in my mind to one – there you
Lie quite absorbed by peace – the calm
Which life could not provide is balm
In death. Unseen by me, you look
Past bed and stairs and half-read book
Eternally upon your home,
The end of pain, the left alone.
I have no friend, or intercessor,
No psychopomp or true confessor
But only you who know my heart
In every cramped and devious part –
Then take my hand and lead me out,
The sky is overcast by doubt,
The time has come, I listen for
Your words of comfort at the door,
O guide me through the shoals of fear –
'Fürchte dich nicht, ich bin bei dir.'

(1975)

→ ←

Ian McEwan (b. 1948) won the 1998 Booker Prize for his novel *Amsterdam*. His other novels range from *The Cement Garden* (1978) and *The Child in Time* (1987) via *Saturday* (2005) and *On Chesil Beach* (2007) to *Sweet Tooth* (2012) and *The Children Act* (2014). Several, notably *The Comfort of Strangers* (1981), *Enduring Love* (1997) and *Atonement* (2001) have been made into films. He has also published short stories, screenplays, children's fiction, an oratorio *Or Shall We Die?* (1983) and an opera libretto, *For You* (2008).

Crusoe in England

ELIZABETH BISHOP (1911–79)

→ ←

ANDREW SOLOMON

The meticulous dryness of this narrator, so bereft of the spirit of adventure even while recalling adventures, seems to catch in the throat of the old man who speaks it. His disdain for his own fame and ingenuity, his decorous irritation, and his exhaustion all seem forbidding, even ugly. And then in the final distich comes the barely contained emotion, sending one back to reread the rest of the poem and to hear in its voice not so much bitterness as restraint. Love is circumstantial; we can love anyone if need be; and losing the one we love is the singular catastrophe. Time does not heal it. Every present moment yearns for even the roughest past. The loneliness of Crusoe's desert island is a desiccated topic, but the aloneness born of Friday's measles is intimate, always fresh.

Crusoe in England

A new volcano has erupted,
the papers say, and last week I was reading
where some ship saw an island being born:
at first a breath of steam, ten miles away;
and then a black fleck – basalt, probably –

rose in the mate's binoculars
and caught on the horizon like a fly.
They named it. But my poor old island's still
un-rediscovered, un-renamable.
None of the books has ever got it right.

Well, I had fifty-two
miserable, small volcanoes I could climb
with a few slithery strides –
volcanoes dead as ash heaps.
I used to sit on the edge of the highest one
and count the others standing up,
naked and leaden, with their heads blown off.
I'd think that if they were the size
I thought volcanoes should be, then I had
become a giant;
and if I had become a giant,
I couldn't bear to think what size
the goats and turtles were,
or the gulls, or the overlapping rollers
 – a glittering hexagon of rollers
closing and closing in, but never quite,
glittering and glittering, though the sky
was mostly overcast.

My island seemed to be
a sort of cloud-dump. All the hemisphere's
left-over clouds arrived and hung
above the craters – their parched throats
were hot to touch.
Was that why it rained so much?

And why sometimes the whole place hissed?
The turtles lumbered by, high-domed,
hissing like teakettles.
(And I'd have given years, or taken a few,
for any sort of kettle, of course.)
The folds of lava, running out to sea,
would hiss. I'd turn. And then they'd prove
to be more turtles.
The beaches were all lava, variegated,
black, red, and white, and gray;
the marbled colors made a fine display.
And I had waterspouts. Oh,
half a dozen at a time, far out,
they'd come and go, advancing and retreating,
their heads in cloud, their feet in moving patches
of scuffed-up white.
Glass chimneys, flexible, attenuated,
sacerdotal beings of glass . . . I watched
the water spiral up in them like smoke.
Beautiful, yes, but not much company.

I often gave way to self-pity.
'Do I deserve this? I suppose I must.
I wouldn't be here otherwise. Was there
a moment when I actually chose this?
I don't remember, but there could have been.'
What's wrong about self-pity, anyway?
With my legs dangling down familiarly
over a crater's edge, I told myself
'Pity should begin at home.' So the more
pity I felt, the more I felt at home.

The sun set in the sea; the same odd sun
rose from the sea,
and there was one of it and one of me.
The island had one kind of everything:
one tree snail, a bright violet-blue
with a thin shell, crept over everything,
over the one variety of tree,
a sooty, scrub affair.
Snail shells lay under these in drifts
and, at a distance,
you'd swear that they were beds of irises.
There was one kind of berry, a dark red.
I tried it, one by one, and hours apart.
Sub-acid, and not bad, no ill effects;
and so I made home-brew. I'd drink
the awful, fizzy, stinging stuff
that went straight to my head
and play my home-made flute
(I think it had the weirdest scale on earth)
and, dizzy, whoop and dance among the goats.
Home-made, home-made! But aren't we all?
I felt a deep affection for
the smallest of my island industries.
No, not exactly, since the smallest was
a miserable philosophy.

Because I didn't know enough.
Why didn't I know enough of something?
Greek drama or astronomy? The books
I'd read were full of blanks;
the poems – well, I tried

reciting to my iris-beds,
'They flash upon that inward eye,
which is the bliss . . .' The bliss of what?
One of the first things that I did
when I got back was look it up.

The island smelled of goat and guano.
The goats were white, so were the gulls,
and both too tame, or else they thought
I was a goat, too, or a gull.
Baa, baa, baa and *shriek, shriek, shriek,*
baa . . . shriek . . . baa . . . I still can't shake
them from my ears; they're hurting now.
The questioning shrieks, the equivocal replies
over a ground of hissing rain
and hissing, ambulating turtles
got on my nerves.
When all the gulls flew up at once, they sounded
like a big tree in a strong wind, its leaves.
I'd shut my eyes and think about a tree,
an oak, say, with real shade, somewhere.
I'd heard of cattle getting island-sick.
I thought the goats were.
One billy-goat would stand on the volcano
I'd christened *Mont d'Espoir* or *Mount Despair*
(I'd time enough to play with names),
and bleat and bleat, and sniff the air.
I'd grab his beard and look at him.
His pupils, horizontal, narrowed up
and expressed nothing, or a little malice.
I got so tired of the very colors!

One day I dyed a baby goat bright red
with my red berries, just to see
something a little different.
And then his mother wouldn't recognize him.

Dreams were the worst. Of course I dreamed of food
and love, but they were pleasant rather
than otherwise. But then I'd dream of things
like slitting a baby's throat, mistaking it
for a baby goat. I'd have
nightmares of other islands
stretching away from mine, infinities
of islands, islands spawning islands,
like frogs' eggs turning into polliwogs
of islands, knowing that I had to live
on each and every one, eventually,
for ages, registering their flora,
their fauna, their geography.

Just when I thought I couldn't stand it
another minute longer, Friday came.
(Accounts of that have everything all wrong.)
Friday was nice.
Friday was nice, and we were friends.
If only he had been a woman!
I wanted to propagate my kind,
and so did he, I think, poor boy.
He'd pet the baby goats sometimes,
and race with them, or carry one around.
  – Pretty to watch; he had a pretty body.

And then one day they came and took us off.

Now I live here, another island,
that doesn't seem like one, but who decides?
My blood was full of them; my brain
bred islands. But that archipelago
has petered out. I'm old.
I'm bored, too, drinking my real tea,
surrounded by uninteresting lumber.
The knife there on the shelf –
it reeked of meaning, like a crucifix.
It lived. How many years did I
beg it, implore it, not to break?
I knew each nick and scratch by heart,
the bluish blade, the broken tip,
the lines of wood-grain on the handle . . .
Now it won't look at me at all.
The living soul has dribbled away.
My eyes rest on it and pass on.

The local museum's asked me to
leave everything to them:
the flute, the knife, the shrivelled shoes,
my shedding goatskin trousers
(moths have got in the fur),
the parasol that took me such a time
remembering the way the ribs should go.
It still will work but, folded up,
looks like a plucked and skinny fowl.
How can anyone want such things?

– And Friday, my dear Friday, died of measles
seventeen years ago come March.

(1976)

→ ←

Andrew Solomon (b.1963) won the 2001 National Book Award
for *The Noonday Demon: An Atlas of Depression*, which was also a
finalist for the Pulitzer Prize and named as one of *The Times*'s one
hundred best books of the decade. His most recent book, *Far from the
Tree: Parents, Children, and the Search for Identity* (2012), received
the National Book Critics Circle Award. An activist in the fields of
mental health, LGBT rights, education and the arts, he is also the
author of *The Irony Tower* (1991) and a novel, *A Stone Boat* (1994),
as well as numerous award-winning articles for major US newspapers,
magazines and academic journals.

For Julia, in the Deep Water

JOHN N. MORRIS (1931–1997)

→ ←

TOBIAS WOLFF

I have raised three children, and lived through this very moment with each of them, not only in watching them learn to swim, but in sending them off for their first day of school – watching them wave uncertainly, bravely, from the window of the vanishing bus; handing them the keys to the car for their first solo run; sending them away to college, to foreign countries, to romance and marriage – learning to stand back, 'doing nothing', as they enter the deep water.

And this poem always makes it happen again for me: that sense of my children needing help, needing me, that helplessness, that desolation of letting go, that joy in their courage, their hunger for all of life's possibilities and hazards. And always the knowledge, sometimes sleeping, sometimes awake, sometimes jangling like an alarm, that in the end they will follow where I am bound, whatever the skill and struggle that has kept us afloat. They will learn to let go, as I am still learning to let go. I never did anything harder.

For Julia, in the Deep Water

The instructor we hire
because she does not love you
Leads you into the deep water,
The deep end
Where the water is darker –
Her open, encouraging arms
That never get nearer
Are merciless for your sake.

You will dream this water always
Where nothing draws nearer,
Wasting your valuable breath
You will scream for your mother –
Only your mother is drowning
Forever in the thin air
Down at the deep end.
She is doing nothing,
She never did anything harder.
And I am beside her.

I am beside her in this imagination.
We are waiting
Where the water is darker.
You are over your head,
Screaming, you are learning
Your way toward us,
You are learning how
In the helpless water
It is with our skill
We live in what kills us.

(1976)

→ ←

The books of Tobias Wolff (b. 1945) include the memoirs *This Boy's Life* (1989) and *In Pharaoh's Army: Memories of the Lost War* (1994); the short novel *The Barracks Thief* (1984); the novel *Old School* (2003); and four collections of short stories, *In the Garden of the North American Martyrs* (1981), *Back in the World* (1985), *The Night in Question* (1997) and, most recently, *Our Story Begins: New and Selected Stories* (2008). He has also edited several anthologies, among them *The Vintage Book of Contemporary American Short Stories* (1994). He is the Ward W. and Priscilla B. Woods Professor in the Humanities at Stanford University.

Aubade

PHILIP LARKIN (1922–85)

→ ←

WILLIAM SIEGHART

Philip Larkin has, amongst his many gifts, an extraordinary ability to embrace a feeling or thought that the rest of us would quickly strike from our mind because it was so disturbing, and examine that thought properly and turn it into a poem. 'Aubade' is the supreme example of this. Waking up in the middle of the night and worrying about one's death is an experience we all can recognise, one that most of us would rather not spend too much time thinking about. Yet Larkin does the opposite and constructs a poem of universal relevance without the conceit of poetic obfuscation. I think it is one of the finest poems written in the last half of the twentieth century and, however many times I read or recite it, the eyes inevitably begin to moisten.

Aubade

I work all day, and get half-drunk at night.
Waking at four to soundless dark, I stare.
In time the curtain-edges will grow light.
Till then I see what's really always there:
Unresting death, a whole day nearer now,
Making all thought impossible but how

And where and when I shall myself die.
Arid interrogation: yet the dread
Of dying, and being dead,
Flashes afresh to hold and horrify.

The mind blanks at the glare. Not in remorse
 – The good not done, the love not given, time
Torn off unused – nor wretchedly because
An only life can take so long to climb
Clear of its wrong beginnings, and may never;
But at the total emptiness for ever,
The sure extinction that we travel to
And shall be lost in always. Not to be here,
Not to be anywhere,
And soon; nothing more terrible, nothing more true.

This is a special way of being afraid
No trick dispels. Religion used to try,
That vast, moth-eaten musical brocade
Created to pretend we never die,
And specious stuff that says *No rational being
Can fear a thing it will not feel,* not seeing
That this is what we fear – no sight, no sound,
No touch or taste or smell, nothing to think with,
Nothing to love or link with,
The anaesthetic from which none come round.

And so it stays just on the edge of vision,
A small, unfocused blur, a standing chill
That slows each impulse down to indecision.
Most things may never happen: this one will,

And realisation of it rages out
In furnace-fear when we are caught without
People or drink. Courage is no good:
It means not scaring others. Being brave
Lets no one off the grave.
Death is no different whined at than withstood.

Slowly light strengthens, and the room takes shape.
It stands plain as a wardrobe, what we know,
Have always known, know that we can't escape,
Yet can't accept. One side will have to go.
Meanwhile telephones crouch, getting ready to ring
In locked-up offices, and all the uncaring
Intricate rented world begins to rouse.
The sky is white as clay, with no sun.
Work has to be done.
Postmen like doctors go from house to house.

(1977)

→ ←

After cofounding Forward Publishing in 1986, the British entrepreneur and philanthropist William Sieghart (b. 1960) launched the influential Forward Prizes for Poetry in 1992 and two years later National Poetry Day, which sees poetry celebrated around the UK each October. In 2012, to mark the London Olympic and Paralympic Games, he launched Winning Words, a public art project to place poetry in public places, as well as editing an anthology of that title.

Dear Bryan Wynter

W. S. GRAHAM (1918–86)

→ ←

NICK LAIRD

I'm not sure any poem has made me cry exactly, but there are many poems I find very moving. Some come to mind immediately: Edward Thomas's 'Rain' or 'Old Man', Zbigniew Herbert's 'Remembering My Father', Heaney's 'Clearances' sequence, Les Murray's 'The Mitchells', Frank O'Hara's 'Having a Coke with You', Rilke's Eighth Elegy, Larkin's 'Aubade', George Herbert's 'The Pearl'. But today I'll opt for W. S. Graham's 'Dear Bryan Wynter', which, along with his poems 'Lines on Roger Hilton's Watch' and 'Private Poem to Norman MacLeod', says something lean and direct about the strengths and limitations of friendship, about how far one can journey from the 'ego house', as Graham calls it in the MacLeod poem, and suggests that poetry, 'a kind / Of news of no time', is a way to practise talking with the dead.

Dear Bryan Wynter
1
This is only a note
To say how sorry I am
You died. You will realise

What a position it puts
Me in. I couldn't really
Have died for you if so
I were inclined. The carn
Foxglove here on the wall
Outside your first house
Leans with me standing
In the Zennor wind.

Anyhow how are things?
Are you still somewhere
With your long legs
And twitching smile under
Your blue hat walking
Across a place? Or am
I greedy to make you up
Again out of memory?
Are you there at all?
I would like to think
You were all right
And not worried about
Monica and the children
And not unhappy or bored.

2

Speaking to you and not
Knowing if you are there
Is not too difficult.
My words are used to that.
Do you want anything?

Where shall I send something?
Rice-wine, meanders, paintings
By your contemporaries?
Or shall I send a kind
Of news of no time
Leaning against the wall
Outside your old house.

The house and the whole moor
Is flying in the mist.

3
I am up. I've washed
The front of my face
And here I stand looking
Out over the top
Half of my bedroom window.
There almost as far
As I can see I see
St Buryan's church tower.
An inch to the left, behind
That dark rise of woods,
Is where you used to lurk.

4
This is only a note
To say I am aware
You are not here. I find
It difficult to go
Beside Housman's star

Lit fences without you.
And nobody will laugh
At my jokes like you.

5

Bryan, I would be obliged
If you would scout things out
For me. Although I am not
Just ready to start out.
I am trying to be better,
Which will make you smile
Under your blue hat.

I know I make a symbol
Of the foxglove on the wall.
It is because it knows you.

(c. 1977)

→ ←

Nick Laird (b. Northern Ireland, 1975) worked as a litigator for several years before leaving to write full-time. He has published three collections of poetry, *To a Fault* (2005), *On Purpose* (2007) and *Go Giants* (2013), and two novels, *Utterly Monkey* (2005) and *Glover's Mistake* (2009). He is a Fellow of the Royal Society of Literature and teaches at Princeton University.

A Meeting

WENDELL BERRY (1934–)

→ ←

COLUM MCCANN

The only person who truly wants to admit to crying over a poem is the poet herself or himself. Most poems don't come like a burning bush or a pillar of light. They are worked and worried into being. But when they finally emerge they should have the appearance of absolute ease. Poets are so much like dancers who ruin their ankles for the sake of a moment's beauty in the air. The fact is that they occasionally soar. So much craft goes into the making of a poem that I imagine most poets would be delighted to learn that someone else, other than themselves, has cried over it. Still, it can happen. And, like most men, I'm more easily moved to tears than I'm prepared to tell anyone. I don't know a poem that consistently brings a tear to my eye, but I can always count on Wendell Berry's 'A Meeting' to create wine from water. It's a beautiful poem, not meant to make us cry, but to celebrate the passing of loved ones. I read it recently at the wake of a good friend. It did indeed make me weep then, though there are other times it simply breaks open the day.

I have developed a favourite thing at Christmastime, where I ask my kids to learn a poem off by heart and 'give' it to me rather than a pair of socks or yet another scarf. It's my favourite moment of the whole year.

I give them a poem and they learn it. Sometimes the poems are wildly different, from 'A Meeting' to 'The Lovesong of J. Alfred Prufrock'. But this Berry poem will always be theirs, and therefore mine.

Berry is a poet who has a singular refusal to engage with the sentimental and yet is always brave enough to engage the necessity of sentiment. We are, all of us, going to end up under some mighty fine trees. All good poems come around to other poems. I suppose the question is, 'Do we dare to eat the peach?' In Berry's world, we always do.

A Meeting

In a dream I meet
my dead friend. He has,
I know, gone long and far,
and yet he is the same
for the dead are changeless.
They grow no older.
It is I who have changed,
grown strange to what I was.
Yet I, the changed one,
ask: 'How you been?'
He grins and looks at me.
'I been eating peaches
off some mighty fine trees.'

(1980)

❧ ❧

The novels of the Irish writer Colum McCann (b. 1965) range from *Fishing the Sloe-Black River* (1994) and *Songdogs* (1995) to *Zoli* (2006), *Let the Great World Spin* (National Book Award, 2009) and *TransAtlantic* (2013). He is Professor of Creative Writing at Hunter College, New York.

eulogy to a hell of a dame –

CHARLES BUKOWSKI (1920–94)

→ ←

MIKE LEIGH

Near the bone. Strikes a chord. Takes me back. Hits a nerve. Brings a lump.

eulogy to a hell of a dame –
some dogs who sleep at night
must dream of bones
and I remember your bones
in flesh
and best
in that dark green dress
and those high-heeled bright
black shoes,
you always cursed when you
drank,
your hair coming down you
wanted to explode out of
what was holding you:
rotten memories of a
rotten
past, and
you finally got

out
by dying,
leaving me with the
rotten
present;
you've been dead
28 years
yet I remember you
better than any of
the rest;
you were the only one
who understood
the futility of the
arrangement of
life;
all the others were only
displeased with
trivial segments,
carped
nonsensically about
nonsense;
Jane, you were
killed by
knowing too much.
here's a drink
to your bones
that
this dog
still
dreams about.

(1984)

→ ←

The television and feature films made by the writer and director Mike Leigh (b. 1943) include *Bleak Moments* (1971), *High Hopes* (1988), *Life Is Sweet* (1990), *Naked* (Best Director, Cannes, 1993), *Secrets and Lies* (winner of the Cannes Palme d'Or, 1996), *Career Girls* (1997), *Topsy-Turvy* (1999), *Vera Drake* (winner of the Venice Film Festival Golden Lion, 2004), *Happy-Go-Lucky* (2008), *Another Year* (2010) and *Mr Turner* (2014). He has also written and directed stage plays including *Abigail's Party* (1977) and, most recently, *Grief* (2011).

Midsummer: 'Sonnet XLIII'

DEREK WALCOTT (1930–)

→ ←

MARK HADDON

I have never much liked sentiment in poetry, and sentimentality is the death knell for pretty much all literature ('One must have a heart of stone to read the death of Little Nell without laughing,' as Oscar Wilde reportedly said). It doesn't happen often, but what moves me most profoundly is the sublime sublimely articulated, a feeling that language has somehow taken me beyond the boundary of language. For obvious reasons it's hard to say precisely how this happens – though Shakespeare's poetry does it most often – but it's close to the feeling I get in certain landscapes or standing under a starry sky on a clear night, a kind of ecstasy which is neither happiness nor sadness nor fear nor contentment but some paradoxical combination of all four.

And Derek Walcott's poem? It's the details, to begin with, the sky flickering like a TV set, those 'teeth broken as dice', the way it then breaks free from history and geography, sweeping us upward to a high, cold point from which we find ourselves looking down on all time and space in the company of an old man for whom it means nothing, who simply turns his pony round and walks away into the endless, white forest.

Midsummer: 'Sonnet XLIII'

Chicago's avenues, as white as Poland.
A blizzard of heavenly coke hushes the ghettos.
The scratched sky flickers like a TV set.
Down Michigan Avenue, slow as the glacial prose
of historians, my taxi crawls. The stalled cars are as frozen
as the faces of cloaked queues on a Warsaw street,
or the hands of black derelicts flexing over a fire-
barrel under the El; above, the punctured sky
is needled by rockets that keep both Empires high.
It will be both ice and fire. In the sibyl's crystal
The globe is shaken with ash, with a child's frisson.
It'll be like this. A bird cry will sound like a pistol
down the avenues. Cars like dead horses, their muzzles
foaming with ice. From the cab's dashboard, a tinny
dispatcher's voice warns of more snow. A picture
lights up the set – first, indecipherable puzzles;
then, in plain black and white, a snow slope with pines
as shaggy as the manes of barbarian ponies;
then, a Mongol in yak's skin, teeth broken as dice,
grinning at the needles of the silent cities
of the plains below him up in the Himalayas,
who slaps the snow from his sides and turns away as,
in lance-like birches, the horde's ponies whinny.

(1984)

→ ←

Mark Haddon (b. 1962) is an author, illustrator and screenwriter who
has written fifteen books for children and won two BAFTAs. His best-
selling novel, *The Curious Incident of the Dog in the Night-time* (2003),

won seventeen literary prizes, including the Whitbread Award, and was staged by the National Theatre. His subsequent publications include a poetry collection, *The Talking Horse and the Sad Girl and the Village Under the Sea* (2005). His most recent novel is *The Red House* (2012).

In Blackwater Woods

MARY OLIVER (1935–)

→ ←

MARC FORSTER

The first thing I did after reading this poem for the first time was to stop. It was like I had been chasing after something and suddenly I just stopped and looked around me. I stopped inside and my mind became peaceful and clear. We don't know what it means to let go. It is very hard to discover that nothing is permanent and we invent numerous beliefs to protect us from the fear of letting go. We are frightened of letting go, because we have postponed it.

To find out what actually takes place when you let go, you must die. Not physically but psychologically, considering yourself dead to all things you have cherished, which is very hard for me. So I started crying at the end of the poem because of my love for life, humanity and stories. Those stories that someone has lived evoke a melancholy emotion of a time gone by. One that you can't hold on to and need to let go. But I believe that only through that act will my mind be free and able to truly experience what true freedom is.

In Blackwater Woods

Look, the trees
are turning
their own bodies
into pillars

of light,
are giving off the rich
fragrance of cinnamon
and fulfillment,

the long tapers
of cattails
are bursting and floating away over
the blue shoulders

of the ponds,
and every pond,
no matter what its
name is, is

nameless now.
Every year
everything
I have ever learned

in my lifetime
leads back to this: the fires
and the black river of loss
whose other side

is salvation,
whose meaning
none of us will ever know.
To live in this world

you must be able
to do three things:
to love what is mortal;
to hold it

against your bones knowing
your own life depends on it;
and, when the time comes to let it go, to let it go.

(1984)

→ ←

The Swiss-German filmmaker and screenwriter Marc Forster (b. 1969) directed *Monster's Ball* (2001), *Finding Neverland* (2004), *Stay* (2005), *Stranger Than Fiction* (2006), *The Kite Runner* (2007) and the twenty-second James Bond film *Quantum of Solace* (2008). His most recent film is *World War Z* (2013), starring Brad Pitt. Forster has also worked with the Red Cross and the Swiss federal health department's HIV prevention campaign.

Love After Love

DEREK WALCOTT (1930–)

→ ←

TOM HIDDLESTON

I read this poem often, once a month at least. In the madness and mayhem of modern life, where every man seems committed to an endless search for the approval and esteem of his fellows and peers, no matter what the cost, this poem reminds me of a basic truth: that we are, as we are, 'enough'. Most of us are motivated deep down by a sense of insufficiency, a need to be better, stronger, faster; to work harder; to be more committed, more kind, more self-sufficient, more successful. We are driven by a sense that we are not, as we are, 'enough'.

But this short poem by Derek Walcott is like a declaration of unconditional love. It's like the embrace of an old friend. We are each of us whole, perfectly imperfect, *enough*. 'Feast on your life' feels like permission, as though Walcott is calling time on all the madness, the mayhem, the insecurity, the neuroses, the drama, and with a big, broad, kind smile, he brings us to an awareness of the present moment, calm and peaceful, and to a feeling of gratitude for everything that we have. I read it to my dearest friends after dinner once, and to my family at Christmas, and they started crying. Which always, unfailingly, makes me cry.

Love After Love

The time will come
when, with elation,
you will greet yourself arriving
at your own door, in your own mirror,
and each will smile at the other's welcome,

and say, sit here. Eat.
You will love again the stranger who was your self.
Give wine. Give bread. Give back your heart
to itself, to the stranger who has loved you

all your life, whom you ignored
for another, who knows you by heart.
Take down the love letters from the bookshelf,

the photographs, the desperate notes,
peel your own image from the mirror.
Sit. Feast on your life.

(c. 1984)

→ ←

The screen roles of Tom Hiddleston (b. 1981) range from F. Scott
Fitzgerald in Woody Allen's *Midnight in Paris* (2011) to Henry V in
the BBC TV Shakespeare series *The Hollow Crown* (2012), Adam
in Jim Jarmusch's *Only Lovers Left Alive* (2013) and the supervillain
Loki in Marvel's *Thor* (2011) and *The Avengers* (2012). He has also
appeared in *Archipelago* (2010), *War Horse* (2011) and *The Deep Blue
Sea* (2011). His stage work includes *Coriolanus* and *Othello* at the
Donmar Warehouse and *Ivanov* (West End).

Extract from *and our faces, my heart, brief as photos*

JOHN BERGER (1926–)

➜ ←

SIMON MCBURNEY

Love joins. Love's opposite is separation. And death separates eternally. It is an unbridgeable gap that we constantly yearn to close as we pledge to love eternally.

'. . . So long lives this and this gives life to thee.'

My father was an archaeologist. He knew about bridging gaps. There were bones he dug which were more fragile than the earth that surrounded them. Shards of flint were reassembled to reveal the hands that knapped them. He uncovered, analysed, and reassembled artefacts, suggesting conjunctions that revealed a truth about our past and joined us with it. This is what John Berger does. He also joins. His tools are words. And in his exquisite book *and our faces, my heart, brief as photos,* he uses these tools to dig like an archaeologist, distil like a chemist, theorise like a cosmologist, excavating in the earth of vulnerable human experience, and then joining the fragments he uncovers with an eye as sure as an astronomer and a hand as gentle as a carpenter. And in this poem, written in prose, he does something extraordinary. He joins love and its enemy separation. He makes, he constructs, a promise. A promise that is, perhaps, indistinguishable from the promise of poetry itself. A promise, as Berger puts it '. . . that language has acknowledged, has given shelter, to the experience which demanded, which cried out.'

> **Extract from** *and our faces, my heart, brief as photos*
> What reconciles me to my own death more than anything
> else is the image of a place: a place where your bones and
> mine are buried, thrown, uncovered, together. They are
> strewn there pell-mell. One of your ribs leans against my
> skull. A metacarpal of my left hand lies inside your pelvis.
> (Against my broken ribs your breast like a flower.) The
> hundred bones of our feet are scattered like gravel. It is
> strange that this image of our proximity, concerning as it does
> mere phosphate of calcium, should bestow a sense of peace.
> Yet it does. With you I can imagine a place where to be phosphate
> of calcium is enough.
>
> (1984)

→ ←

The actor, writer, and director Simon McBurney (b. 1957) cofounded the theatre company Complicité in 1983 and remains its artistic director. His productions for the company include *The Elephant Vanishes* (2003), *A Disappearing Number* (2007) and *The Master and Margarita* (2012). He has also directed Broadway productions of *The Resistible Rise of Arturo Ui*, starring Al Pacino (2002), and *All My Sons* (2008). He has acted in films such as *The Last King of Scotland* (2006) and *Tinker Tailor Soldier Spy* (2011), and in the television comedies *The Vicar of Dibley* and *Rev*. His publications include a volume of essays, *Who You Hear It From* (2012).

Sandra's Mobile

DOUGLAS DUNN (1942-)

➔ ⬅

RICHARD EYRE

There are not many poems about death which don't carry some baggage about the life eternal or, in offering comfort, offer advertisements for religious consolation. What moves me so much about Douglas Dunn's poem – which comes from a collection called *Elegies*, all relating to the death of his wife – is that it's about love and the survival of love.

Sandra's Mobile
A constant artist, dedicated to
Curves, shapes, the pleasant shades, the feel of colour,
She did not care what shapes, what red, what blue,
Scorning the dull to ridicule the duller
With a disinterested, loyal eye.
So Sandra brought her this and taped it up –
Three seagulls from a white and indoor sky –
A gift of old artistic comradeship.
'Blow on them, Love.' Those silent birds winged round
On thermals of my breath. On her last night,
Trying to stay awake, I saw love crowned

In tears and wooden birds and candlelight.
She did not wake again. To prove our love
Each gull, each gull, each gull, turned into dove.

(1985)

➔ ◆

Director of Britain's National Theatre from 1987 to 1997, Sir Richard Eyre (b. 1943) has won numerous awards including five Oliviers for productions ranging from *Guys and Dolls* to Tom Stoppard's *The Invention of Love*. His film credits include *Iris* (2001), *Notes on a Scandal* (2006) and *The Other Man* (2008). His opera productions include *Carmen* for the Metropolitan Opera, New York, 2010.

Brindis con el Viejo

MAURICIO ROSENCOF (1933–)

✦ ✦

JUAN MÉNDEZ

I read this sonnet only in 2012, although for decades I had known the story of the inhumane conditions in which the Uruguayan 'hostages' were held for eleven years. Coming at the very end of the remarkable *Memorias del Calabozo*, the poem brought tears to my eyes because it made me think of my own father and his unyielding moral support for me when I was a political prisoner in Argentina. I remembered also how I imagined my dad's sadness and at times distress, as I spent my days in a cell under conditions that could change for the worse at any time. They did for several friends of mine and I can only imagine the despair of their own fathers.

The poem is written in the familiar Spanish of the River Plate and it describes a Sunday ritual that is very common to families in the Southern Cone of South America. My father was also fond of a drink with family before a Sunday luncheon. He preferred vermouth to grappa, but the effect is the same: an opportunity to share a loving ritual with offspring and to share the events of the week and plans for the future with sons, daughters, and grandkids. When those moments are rendered impossible by prison or exile, their remembrance stings with nostalgia, guilt, and love.

Brindis con el Viejo

Yo sé que los domingos, casi al mediodía,
Abrís con cautela el viejo aparador,
Y vertís en un vaso el mismo licor
Que en los buenos tiempos con vos compartía.
Yo sé que a ese trago le falta alegría
Y que al tomarlo no le hallás sabor,
Porque a veces suele borrar el dolor
Su gusto al vino y la luz al día.
Pero vos sabés que la tormenta pasa
Y que el implacable sol no se detiene
Cuando un nefasto nubarrón lo tapa.
Por eso sé que volveré a tu casa
Algún domingo que el almanaque tiene,
Para beber con vos una risueña grapa.

(C. 1987)

Raising a Glass with My Old Man

I know that on Sundays, at around midday,
You cautiously open the ancient sideboard
And pour a glass of the same grape liquor
We used to share in better times.
I know you're not happy now when you drink it,
That it's lost all savor for you,
Because sometimes sorrow can quite erase
One's taste for wine and the light of day.
But you know, as I do, that the storm will pass
And that the implacable sun doesn't simply stop
When obscured by a dark, pernicious cloud,
Which is why I know I'll return to your house –

On a Sunday that's there on the calendar –
And laugh with you over a glass of grappa.

TRANSLATION BY MARGARET JULL COSTA

→ ←

The Argentine-born human rights lawyer Juan Méndez (b. 1944) was adopted as an Amnesty International 'Prisoner of Conscience' in the mid-1970s after his arrest, imprisonment and torture by the Argentinean regime for representing political prisoners. Now based in the United States, he launched Human Rights Watch's Americas Program, has served as president of the International Center for Transitional Justice and is currently the United Nations Special Rapporteur on torture.

An End or a Beginning

BEI DAO (1949-)

→ ←

WUER KAIXI

Bei Dao, one of the leading thinkers in my generation, enlightened tens if not hundreds of millions of Chinese with his poems. In the time of the Cultural Revolution or the years following it, the people of China had long forgotten the ability to think independently. With his words, Bei Dao truly showed us that concepts like integrity, honesty, courage and, most of all, the longing for freedom are so beautiful and worth living for, worth fighting for, worth crying for.

I came across his poems when I was a teenager. It was the 1980s in China, when people were waking up. Yet one thing the regime did not want to stir in the deeply hibernating minds of the people was the consciousness of independence. His words, particularly these lines from his celebrated poem 'An End or a Beginning' – 'If fresh blood could make you fertile / The ripened fruit / On tomorrow's branches / Would bear my colour' – brought tears to my sixteen-year-old eyes, and have kept the flame of ideas kindled in my heart.

An End or a Beginning

(for Yu Luoke)

Here I stand
Replacing another, who has been murdered
So that each time the sun rises
A heavy shadow, like a road
Shall run across the land

A sorrowing mist
Covers the uneven patchwork of roofs
Between one house and another
Chimneys spout ashy crowds
Warmth effuses from gleaming trees
Lingering on the wretched cigarette stubs
Low black clouds arise
From every tired hand

In the name of the sun
Darkness plunders openly
Silence is still the story of the East
People on age-old frescoes
Silently live forever
Silently die and are gone

Ah, my beloved land
Why don't you sing any more
Can it be true that even the ropes of the Yellow River
    towmen
Like sundered lute-strings

Reverberate no more
True that time, this dark mirror
Has also turned its back on you forever
Leaving only stars and drifting clouds behind

I look for you
In every dream
Every foggy night or morning
I look for spring and apple trees
Every wisp of breeze stirred up by honey bees
I look for the seashore's ebb and flow
The seagulls formed from sunlight on the waves
I look for the stories built into the wall
Your forgotten name and mine

If fresh blood could make you fertile
The ripened fruit
On tomorrow's branches
Would bear my colour

I must admit
That I trembled
In the death-white chilly light
Who wants to be a meteorite
Or a martyr's ice-cold statue
Watching the unextinguished fire of youth
Pass into another's hand
Even if doves alight on its shoulder
It can't feel their bodies' warmth and breath
They preen their wings
And quickly fly away

I am a man
I need love
I long to pass each tranquil dusk
Under my love's eyes
Waiting in the cradle's rocking
For the child's first cry
On the grass and fallen leaves
On every sincere gaze
I write poems of life
This universal longing
Has now become the whole cost of being a man

I have lied many times
In my life
But I have always honestly kept to
The promise I made as a child
So that the world which cannot tolerate
A child's heart
Has still not forgiven me

Here I stand
Replacing another, who has been murdered
I have no other choice
And where I fall
Another will stand
A wind rests on my shoulders
Stars glimmer in the wind

Perhaps one day
The sun will become a withered wreath
To hand before

The growing forest of gravestones
Of each unsubmitting fighter
Black crows the night's tatters
Flock thick around

(1986)

TRANSLATION BY BONNIE S. MCDOUGALL

→ ←

Wuer Kaixi (b. 1968) was the Chinese student of Uyghur ethnicity who led the human rights protests in Tiananmen Square in 1989. After publicly confronting Premier Li Peng on national television, he was put on China's 'most wanted' list and fled through Hong Kong to France and the United States, where he studied at Harvard University. He now lives in Taiwan, where he works as a political commentator, and continues his endeavours for freedom in China.

A Call

SEAMUS HEANEY (1939-2013)

→ ←

RICHARD CURTIS

As my father grew older, I noticed that he rarely came close to shedding tears about the sad and serious things in our lives. But if ever telling a tale of something good, some gracious or loving piece of behaviour, tears would always come into his eyes. And I feel myself going that way as I too get older. Sadness somehow I expect. Kindness and love take me by surprise. So I love this poem with its bold and unexpected simple statement of love in the final line.

It also moves me because I have always presumed it is a poem about a friend – and I have failed my friends, mainly, and failed to fulfil the potential of my friendships, allowing the other big things in my life to edge them out. So it's also very much a poem about my life – and the fact that the author almost says I love you, but doesn't – well, there's the sadness in it, after all . . .

A Call

'Hold on,' she said, 'I'll just run out and get him.
The weather here's so good, he took the chance
To do a bit of weeding.'

So I saw him
Down on his hands and knees beside the leek rig,
Touching, inspecting, separating one
Stalk from the other, gently pulling up
Everything not tapered, frail and leafless,
Pleased to feel each little weed-root break,
But rueful also . . .

Then found myself listening to
The amplified grave ticking of hall clocks
Where the phone lay unattended in a calm
Of mirror glass and sunstruck pendulums . . .

And found myself then thinking: if it were nowadays,
This is how Death would summon Everyman.

Next thing he spoke and I nearly said I loved him.

(c. 1987)

→ ←

The screenwriter and director Richard Curtis (b. 1956) is best known for such romantic comedy films as *Four Weddings and a Funeral* (1994), *Notting Hill* (1999), *Bridget Jones's Diary* (2001), *Love Actually* (2003) and *About Time* (2013), as well as the TV series *Blackadder* and *Mr. Bean*. He is also the cofounder of the British charity Comic Relief.

Extract from 'Eastern War Time'

ADRIENNE RICH (1929–2012)

➤ ◄

ANISH KAPOOR

This poem describes the atrocities of war from the position of an American girl who remains 'ignorantly Jewish'. Rich tangles the reader between identification and innocence, and suggests that memory, even our sense of humanity, can be confused by trauma, 'Memory says: want to do right? Don't count on me.' Reading this poem jogs a sense of the indirect guilt we feel when we are faced with the plight of humanity and our own inability or unwillingness to act. In an extraordinary political description of empathy and compassion, Rich imagines 'I'm a field with corners left for the landless.'

We are called to stand alongside the poet and dream of 'world revolution', and invited to 'stand on the road to Ramallah with naked face.' The incantation 'I'm a corpse dredged from a canal in Berlin' makes me and my body the field of action. I can't read these lines without tears in my eyes. What do I sell when 'I'm the woman who sells for a boat ticket', when 'I'm a woman bargaining for a chicken'? The fragility of the individual is present as victim and perpetrator – what is right and wrong in the midst of desperation, when 'I'm accused of child – death'? Rich makes us fully present – 'I am standing here in your poem'. Each one of us is not innocent but 'unsatisfied / lifting my smoky mirror'. This most political of poems is deeply intimate and gives us no escape from the humanity of suffering and loss.

Eastern War Time
10
Memory says: Want to do right? Don't count on me.
I'm a canal in Europe where bodies are floating
I'm a mass grave   I'm the life that returns
I'm a table set with room for the Stranger
I'm a field with corners left for the landless
I'm accused of child-death   of drinking blood
I'm a man-child praising God   he's a man
I'm a woman bargaining for a chicken
I'm a woman who sells for a boat ticket
I'm a family dispersed between night and fog
I'm an immigrant tailor who says *A coat*
is not a piece of cloth only   I sway
in the learnings of the master-mystics
I have dreamed of Zion.   I've dreamed of world revolution
I have dreamed my children could live at last like others
I have walked the children of others through ranks of hatred
I'm a corpse dredged from a canal in Berlin
a river in Mississippi.   I'm a woman standing
with other women dressed in black
on the streets of Haifa, Tel Aviv, Jerusalem
there is spit on my sleeve there are phonecalls in the night
I am a woman standing in line for gasmasks
I stand on a road in Ramallah   with naked face   listening
I am standing here in your poem   unsatisfied
lifting my smoky mirror

(1989–1990)

→ ←

The Indian-born British sculptor Anish Kapoor (b. 1954) represented Britain at the 1990 Venice Biennale and won the Turner Prize the following year. His work is now represented in major collections all over the world. Major public works include *Cloud Gate* in Chicago's Millennium Park, *Sky Mirror* (New York 2006, London 2010), *Orbit* (2012 London Olympic Games) and a granite monument in New York's Hanover Square to commemorate the British victims of 11 September 2001.

It Is Here (for A)

HAROLD PINTER (1930–2008)

➜ ⬱

NEIL LABUTE

When you think of 'warm and fuzzy', I can't imagine that Harold Pinter would be the first writer to come to mind (and I don't suppose that I would be in the top ten, either), but that might've been before reading a few of the poems he wrote to his beloved Antonia Fraser.

In his lovely and deceptively simple verses that make up 'It Is Here (for A)', Pinter reveals yearning, fear and desire in a way that would make his more romantic predecessors tear up and blubber away (if you can read the line 'it was the breath we took when we first met' without your eyes misting over, then you're a better man than I am, Gunga Din).

I admire the strength, the muscle, the menace of Pinter's language in his plays and screenplays but a poem like this – written as a memory about the time when he and Lady Antonia first met (and her own favourite poem of his) – makes me love him as the very human creature that he was. Flawed, brilliant, irascible, but gifted with a huge and feeling heart.

This poem makes me cry and makes me want to be a better man – it also moves me for very special reasons as well, and that is all you can ever ask of a few words artfully arranged on an empty slip of paper.

It Is Here (for A)

What sound was that?
I turn away, into the shaking room.

What was that sound that came in on the dark?
What is this maze of light it leaves us in?
What is this stance we take,
To turn away and then turn back?
What did we hear?

It was the breath
we took when we first met.
Listen. It is here.

(1990)

→ ←

The film director, screenwriter and playwright Neil LaBute (b. 1963) first came to prominence with *In the Company of Men* (1997). His subsequent credits include writing and directing *Your Friends and Neighbors* (1998), *The Shape of Things* (2003) and *Some Velvet Morning* (2013) as well as such plays as *The Mercy Seat* (2002), *Fat Pig* (2005), *reasons to be pretty* (2008) and *In a Forest Dark and Deep* (2011). He is also the author of the short story collection *Seconds of Pleasure* (2004).

For Andrew Wood

JAMES FENTON (1949–)

→ ←

DAVID REMNICK

When I was younger I used to read a great deal of contemporary American and English poetry. I still do. But I also used to go to readings, which I no longer have as much time for. Ginsberg, Snyder, Levertov, Robert Hass, Louise Glück . . . The best was Joseph Brodsky, a cross between Akhmatova and the Kol Nidre. Years went by without going to hear more, which is a foolish self-deprivation. I had an excuse, I told myself. Too often poets read in a fashionable lament, humourless or blandly incantatory. But then, about fifteen years ago, I went to hear James Fenton, a favourite of mine, at Columbia University. He was extraordinary. In the Russian way, he knew his work by heart and, as he paced the stage like the caged beast in the Kafka story, he seemed to radiate that language, to exude it rather than read or perform it; the language came up from inside his deepest self. Years went by. Then, on 20 April 2012, I went to a memorial service for Christopher Hitchens at Cooper Union. And, because Hitchens was Hitchens, there were wonderfully ribald anecdotes of two-thirds-true journalistic escapades, well-lubricated evenings of talk and friendship. And then there was Fenton, who stepped to the microphone, all business, but clearly shaken, and recited this poem, a poem that had been published years

254

before in *The New York Review of Books*. It was not written for Christopher, but it was revived and recited for him, the perfect lament for the lost friend. I think of it, and am shaken by its rhythms, by James's inimitable voice, every time a friend of mine is lost or in danger of being lost to the thing that consumes us all sooner or later. I couldn't be more grateful for a work of art, for a sustaining, insistent voice.

For Andrew Wood

What would the dead want from us
Watching from their cave?
Would they have us forever howling?
Would they have us rave
Or disfigure ourselves, or be strangled
Like some ancient emperor's slave?

None of my dead friends were emperors
With such exorbitant tastes
And none of them were so vengeful
As to have all their friends waste
Waste quite away in sorrow
Disfigured and defaced.

I think the dead would want us
To weep for what *they* have lost.
I think that our luck in continuing
Is what would affect them most.
But time would find them generous
And less self-engrossed.

And time would find them generous
As they used to be

And what else would they want from us
But an honored place in our memory,
A favorite room, a hallowed chair,
Privilege and celebrity?

And so the dead might cease to grieve
And we might make amends
And there might be a pact between
Dead friends and living friends.
What our dead friends would want from us
Would be such living friends.

(1993)

→ ←

Formerly Moscow correspondent of the *Washington Post*, David Remnick (b. 1958) has been editor of *The New Yorker* since 1998. His six books include the Pulitzer Prize-winning *Lenin's Tomb: The Last Days of the Soviet Empire* (1993) and *The Bridge: The Life and Rise of Barack Obama* (2010).

Not Cancelled Yet

JOHN UPDIKE (1932–2009)

→ ←

JOSEPH O'NEILL

I first read this poem in the days following the news of John Updike's death in January 2009, and I had the confused idea that it belonged to the brief, light snowfall of verse that came from him during his final hospitalisation. In fact, he wrote the poem some fifteen years before, at around the age of sixty. He could equally have written it at age twenty or thirty: Updike seems never to have been free of either mortal dread or, to flip the coin, of an intense love of being alive – a love that extends, in this poem, to the bittersweet taste of a postage stamp on the tongue that licks it. Updike's poems usually bounce off a hard spot in my sensibility – they're a touch trifling, as he would have happily admitted – but this one is wonderful and terrifying.

Not Cancelled Yet
Some honorary day
if I play my cards right
I might be a postage stamp
but I won't be there to lick me
and licking is what I liked,
in tasty anticipation of

the long dark slither from the mailbox,

from box to pouch to hand

to bag to box to slot to hand:

that box is best

whose lid slams open as well as shut,

admitting a parcel of daylight,

the green top of a tree,

and a flickering of fingers, letting go.

(1993)

→ ←

A qualified barrister, who practised in London for ten years while writing his first two novels, the Irish-born, New York-resident Joseph O'Neill (b. 1964) is the author of *Netherland*, which was named as one of the *New York Times'* Ten Best Books of 2008 and won the 2009 PEN/Faulkner Award for Fiction and *The Dog* (2014). He has also written a work of nonfiction, *Blood-Dark Track: A Family History*, as well as literary and cultural criticism, and teaches at Bard College in New York.

Armada

BRIAN PATTEN (1946–)

→ ←

PAUL BETTANY

I was introduced to Brian Patten's work at the age of twenty and since then his poems have kept me company. In real life we are twenty-five years apart, but I always meet him in a place where we are both the same age. The love poems he wrote forty years ago saw me through my twenties, and now the poems he wrote in his forties speak to me with an equal resonance.

'Armada' is a poem about the death of his mother, but it's also about the importance of time and the insignificance of the days and weeks and years with which we measure it.

When I read it I usually start crying at the line 'I kneel beside your bed' and continue howling until its perfect end. It's then that I think of my own childhood and my own children, and how ironic and awful it is – and yet right and proper – that they should take my love for granted. That sort of love can only be fully understood in hindsight.

Reading Brian Patten's poetry does that trick that art should do, which is to sort of adhere you to the surface of the planet, just long enough that you don't go spinning off into the loneliness of space – 'somebody else has felt this too,' you think. And you breathe a little easier.

Armada

Long, long ago
when everything I was told was believable
and the little I knew was less limited than now,
I stretched belly down on the grass beside a pond
and to the far bank launched a child's armada.
A broken fortress of twigs,
the paper-tissue sails of galleons,
the waterlogged branches of submarines –
all came to ruin and were on flame
in that dusk-red pond.
And you, mother, stood behind me,
impatient to be going,
old at twenty-three, alone,
thin overcoat flapping.
How closely the past shadows us.
In a hospital a mile or so from that pond
I kneel beside your bed and, closing my eyes,
reach out across forty years to touch once more
that pond's cool surface,
and it is your cool skin I'm touching;
for as on a pond a child's paper boat
was blown out of reach
by the smallest gust of wind,
so too have you been blown out of reach
by the smallest whisper of death,
and a childhood memory is sharpened,
and the heart burns as that armada burnt,
long, long ago.

(1996)

→ ←

Paul Bettany (b. 1971) first came to prominence in the film *Gangster No. 1* (2000). He has gone on to appear in a wide variety of other films, including *A Beautiful Mind* (2001), *Master and Commander: The Far Side of the World* (2003), *Dogville* (2003), *The Da Vinci Code* (2006), *Margin Call* (2011) and *Avengers: The Age of Ultron* (2015).

A Poetry Reading at West Point

WILLIAM MATTHEWS (1942–1997)

→ ←

TOM MCCARTHY

My wife, who is also a poet, introduced me to this poem. She knows poems and she knows me. Of course it moved me. How could it not? The idea of how people struggle to connect with art also deeply resonates with me. And how the artist struggles to connect with his audience and remain true to . . . well, the truth. Regardless of the side you play for, citizen or artist, the need to reach out, to connect, to feel and to affect is so satisfying and so elusive. The process is awkward, moving, funny, clumsy, desperate and occasionally wondrous. It's essentially human.

'Sir, thank you. Sir.' Straight to my heart.

A Poetry Reading at West Point
I read to the entire plebe class,
in two batches. Twice the hall filled
with bodies dressed alike, each toting
a copy of my book. What would my
shrink say, if I had one, about
such a dream, if it were a dream?

Question and answer time.
'Sir,' a cadet yelled from the balcony,
and gave his name and rank, and then,
closing his parentheses, yelled
'Sir' again. 'Why do your poems give
me a headache when I try

to understand them?' he asked. 'Do
you want that?' I have a gift for
gentle jokes to defuse tension,
but this was not the time to use it.
'I try to write as well as I can
what it feels like to be human,'

I started, picking my way care-
fully, for he and I were, after
all, pained by the same dumb longings.
'I try to say what I don't know
how to say, but of course I can't
get much of it down at all.'

By now I was sweating bullets.
'I don't want my poems to be hard,
unless the truth is, if there is
a truth.' Silence hung in the hall
like a heavy fabric. My own
head ached. 'Sir,' he yelled. 'Thank you. Sir.'

(1997)

→ ←

The actor, screenwriter and director Tom McCarthy (b. 1966) wrote and directed the films *The Station Agent (2003), The Visitor (2007), Win Win (2011)* and *The Cobbler* (2014). His other screenplays include *Up* (2009) and *Million Dollar Arm* (2014). His numerous acting credits include *Meet the Parents* (2000), *Syriana* (2005), *Goodnight, and Good Luck* (2005) and *The Wire* (2008).

Bedecked

VICTORIA REDEL (1959–)

→ ←

BILLY COLLINS

I'm a grown man who reads a lot of poetry, but I cannot recall a single instance of being moved by a poem to sobbing – I mean shoulders shaking, face-in-the-hands sobbing. If a poem begins to show signs that it might have me that way, there's no time for me to break down emotionally. I'm too busy trying to figure out how the poet is managing to pull it off. But there is one reliable test of a poem's power to unglue me – all I have to do is read it out loud to a class. After decades of teaching poetry, I can count on one hand the poems that I find impossible to deliver to a room full of students without losing it; Victoria Redel's 'Bedecked,' I have repeatedly discovered, is one of them.

Redel's poem is a mother's defence of her young son's freedom to dress up whichever way he likes – including lots of accessories – as he innocently flouts the conventions of 'boy' and 'girl' dress. The subject is interesting on its own, but the power of the poem lies in its direct address to its readers, the repeated 'Tell me's', and the escalating determination of the mother to make her point. Judiciously, while she is protecting her son's freedom of appearance, Redel is also granting the reader his or her freedom of speech. You can tell me whatever you like, the mother allows, whatever 'you *need* to tell me'. But then comes the poem's fierce turn: 'but keep far away from my son', with its threatening implication of the reader. But as the poem begins to end, Redel's joyful display of how beauty's 'facets set off prisms' that 'spin up everywhere' as rainbows are cast from the boy's 'jeweled body' is more than enough to convince us that 'it's fine – really maybe even a good thing – a boy who's got some girl to him'. The poem's timing is perfect; its very last word is where tears are likely to overspill their little banks.

Bedecked

Tell me it's wrong the scarlet nails my son sports or the toy
store rings he clusters four jewels to each finger.

He's bedecked. I see the other mothers looking at the star
choker, the rhinestone strand he fastens over a sock.
Sometimes I help him find sparkle clip-ons when he says
sticker earrings look too fake.

Tell me I should teach him it's wrong to love the glitter that a
boy's only a boy who'd love a truck with a remote that revs,
battery slamming into corners or Hot Wheels loop-de-looping
off tracks into the tub.

Then tell me it's fine – really – maybe even a good thing – a boy
who's got some girl to him,
and I'm right for the days he wears a pink shirt on the seesaw in
the park.

Tell me what you need to tell me but keep far away from my son
who still loves a beautiful thing not for what it means –

this way or that – but for the way facets set off prisms and
prisms spin up everywhere
and from his own jeweled body he's cast rainbows – made every
shining true color.

Now try to tell me – man or woman – your heart was ever once
that brave.

(2002)

➔ ◆

Billy Collins (b. 1941) has served two terms as US Poet Laureate. His
latest collection of poems, his fourteenth, is *Aimless Love: New and
Selected Poems 2003–13*.

The Lanyard

BILLY COLLINS (1941–)

→ ←

J. J. ABRAMS

I am the most recent poetry fan in the family. My wife, Katie, however, has long been a true lover of the form; she reads poetry every day, even edits volumes of her favourite works. It comes easy to her in a way it never really did to me.

Except once.

Years ago, listening to NPR on my car radio, I heard Billy Collins (at the time our country's Poet Laureate) recite one of his poems entitled 'The Lanyard'. It gripped me in a way that poetry never had before. It was funny. It was relatable and profound and as I was driving down Washington Boulevard I had tears in my eyes.

'The Lanyard' is about the impossibility of ever paying back the ultimate gift a mother bestows upon a child. I loved it so much I got a copy and gave it to my mom, who loved it as well. Months later, in classic my mom form, she gave me a framed copy of the poem which she had somehow gotten signed by Mr Collins himself.

Katie and I have since been lucky enough to see Billy Collins perform his work in person. I have come to appreciate and, dare I say, even understand poetry, and now officially consider myself a convert.

This poem will always be one of my favourites. By sharing it with my mother, who has since passed away, I was able to at least acknowledge the fact that I could never repay her for all she did for me. Her getting the framed poem for me was her way of saying I never had to. Loving her was enough.

The Lanyard
The other day I was ricocheting slowly
off the blue walls of this room,
moving as if underwater from typewriter to piano,
from bookshelf to an envelope lying on the floor,
when I found myself in the L section of the dictionary
where my eyes fell upon the word lanyard.

No cookie nibbled by a French novelist
could send one into the past more suddenly –
a past where I sat at a workbench at a camp
by a deep Adirondack lake
learning how to braid long thin plastic strips
into a lanyard, a gift for my mother.

I had never seen anyone use a lanyard
or wear one, if that's what you did with them,
but that did not keep me from crossing
strand over strand again and again
until I had made a boxy
red and white lanyard for my mother.

She gave me life and milk from her breasts,
and I gave her a lanyard.
She nursed me in many a sick room,

lifted spoons of medicine to my lips,
laid cold face-cloths on my forehead,
and then led me out into the airy light

and taught me to walk and swim,
and I, in turn, presented her with a lanyard.
Here are thousands of meals, she said,
and here is clothing and a good education.
And here is your lanyard, I replied,
which I made with a little help from a counselor.

Here is a breathing body and a beating heart,
strong legs, bones and teeth,
and two clear eyes to read the world, she whispered,
and here, I said, is the lanyard I made at camp.
And here, I wish to say to her now,
is a smaller gift – not the worn truth

that you can never repay your mother,
but the rueful admission that when she took
the two-tone lanyard from my hand,
I was as sure as a boy could be
that this useless, worthless thing I wove
out of boredom would be enough to make us even.

(2005)

➔ ⬅

J. J. Abrams (b. 1966) is the director of the feature films *Mission: Impossible III* (2006), *Star Trek* (2009), *Super 8* (2011), which he also wrote, and *Star Trek Into Darkness* (2013). His next film as a director will be *Star Wars: Episode VII*. Founder and president of Bad Robot Productions, Abrams also produced the films *Cloverfield* (2008) and *Mission: Impossible – Ghost Protocol* (2011). His television credits as producer and/or creator include *Felicity*, *Alias*, *Lost*, *Fringe*, *Person of Interest* and *Revolution*.

Regarding the home of
one's childhood, one could:

EMILY ZINNEMANN (1984–)

→ ←

COLIN FIRTH

Emily Zinnemann graduated from the University of Toronto and received an MFA from the University of Michigan. I heard this poem at a public reading she gave at the University of Michigan in 2009.

I'm reluctant to talk across this poem; I think it says itself perfectly. It offers sparse, beautiful fragments of memory, and then seems simultaneously to take them away. The unpunctuated ending – as if she's just walked away altogether.

Regarding the Home of One's Childhood, One Could:
forget the plum tree;
forget its black-skinned plums;

    also the weight
    of their leaning as they leaned

        over starry hedges;
        also the hedges,

the dew that turned them starry;
                the wet-bellied pups who slunk there

        trailing ludicrous pedigrees;
                even the eyes

                of birds
                glittering

                in the branches;
                even the branches

→ ←

Colin Firth (b. 1960) won an Academy Award in 2011 for his por-
trayal of King George VI in *The King's Speech*. After coming to
prominence as Mr Darcy in a BBC adaptation of *Pride and Prejudice*
(1995), he has starred in such films as the *Bridget Jones's Diary* series,
A Single Man (2009) and *Tinker Tailor Soldier Spy* (2011).

For Ruthie Rogers in Venice

CRAIG RAINE (1944–)

→ ←

RICHARD ROGERS

A month after the sudden death of our son, Bo, we went to Venice on the weekend of what would have been his twenty-eighth birthday. It is a city we love and know well – we had often gone with our children for summer holidays, and in fact we had just been a few months previously with Bo. We also chose Venice as we had no friends there and we craved a quiet time together.

What we were unprepared for was how the sad winter light and wet weather of the city reflected our mood, and how comforting that was to us. The summer San Marco full of joy, where we would sit with our ice creams or Camparis in the Caffè Florian, was now empty, the hot sun replaced by light rain and grey skies, with wooden walkways ready to take people as the waters rose.

Our time was spent only with each other until the afternoon we met our friend Craig Raine, the poet, and his wife, Ann Pasternak Slater. The four of us sought refuge in the Caffè Quadri and over hot chocolate we talked of Venice and of Bo. A few weeks later Craig sent us this poem – a poem that makes me cry.

For Ruthie Rogers in Venice

(Bo Rogers died November 2011, aged 27)

Shoulders to cry on,
these mooring posts,
trios leaning together,
supporting each other:
in grief and inconsolable.

Mooring posts tapering to blunt black
like a lost child's lost crayons.

The endless wash
of salt water.
See-through, threadbare, worn,

these great fogs like ghosts
in slow flight from some slaughter.

The hoarse cries of fog-horns,
lost in their loss,
with no way back,

and the world gone white
in a single night.

(2012)

→ ←

Richard Rogers (b. 1933) is the 2007 Pritzker Architecture Prize Laureate and the recipient of the 1985 RIBA Gold Medal. He was knighted in 1991 and made a life peer in 1996. His practice, Rogers Stirk Harbour + Partners, is best known for such pioneering buildings as the Centre Georges Pompidou, Paris, the headquarters for Lloyd's of London and Terminal 4 at the Madrid–Barajas Airport. His wife Ruth, to whom the poem is addressed, is the chef and food writer who founded London's River Café.

Keys to the Doors

ROBIN ROBERTSON (1955-)

→ ←

MOHSIN HAMID

I don't go looking for poems. I just find them. (Or they find me.) Like the time some fifteen years ago, sitting in a Manhattan subway car, I looked up and saw, as part of a series called 'Poetry in Motion', lines about longing by Faiz Ahmed Faiz, a poet from my native city of Lahore, and was struck by a sense of, simultaneously, homesickness and being at home.

Three years ago I found 'Keys to the Doors' in a copy of *The New York Review of Books*, mailed to my house in Lahore, and I cut it out and taped it to my printer. It's there now, stirring to the beat of my ceiling fan, as I write this.

I was a father then, am doubly so today, with a daughter coming up on five and a son of two; but then I was a newer father, with a daughter just starting to chat. She'd stride into my room while I was novel-writing, and talk to me, and ask me questions, and bring her fantasies into where I sat draped in mine.

And this poem, this poem for me is that.

Keys to the Doors

for Eilidh

I loved your age of wonder: your third and fourth
and fifth years spent astonished, widening your eyes
at each new trick of the world – and me standing there,
solemnly explaining how it was done. The moon and stars,
rainbows, photographs, gravity, the birds in the air,
the difference between blood and water.
In true life? you would say, looking up
and I would nod, like some broken-hearted sage,
knowing there would be no answers soon
to all the big questions that were left, to cruelty and fear,
to age and grief and death, and no words either.
And you, like me, will sit and shake your head.
In true life? Yes, my sweet, strong daughter, I'm afraid
there is all this as well, and this is it: true life.

(2012)

→ ←

The novels by the Pakistani writer Mohsin Hamid (b. 1971) are *Moth Smoke* (2000), *The Reluctant Fundamentalist* (2007, subsequently turned into a feature film directed by Mira Nair) and *How to Get Filthy Rich in Rising Asia* (2013).

Afterword

NADINE GORDIMER

Pablo Neruda's line: 'Whoever discovers who I am will discover who you are.' I am not a man, neither will be the many women who read and receive the revelations of these poems. But in the lives of the great Neruda and other poets harvested here – whoever you are, man, woman or any other gender – you will discover in yourself matchlessly conveyed the exultation and devastation of human experience. No matter that of the almost a hundred poets chosen by various individuals, only a dozen are women. Neither gender nor the historical era in which the poem was written makes out-of-date the emotions they divulge, even if the vocabulary, 'thees' and 'thous', is at times archaic. Passion of love and loss, morality of 'just war,' the purposeful trajectory of life and its frustrations have been, are, for always.

Here are a few of those poems that moved me most.

Wordsworth, 'Surprised By Joy'

'impatient as the Wind / I turned to share the transport – Oh! With whom. / But thee, long buried in the silent tomb . . . but how could I forget thee? . . . knowing my heart's best treasure was no more.' The terrifying paradox of remembrance.

Shelley, *The Masque of Anarchy*

The brutality of the title refers not to the anarchy of protest but to brutality of politicians who put it down. 'Like Oppression's thundering doom / ringing through each heart and brain / Heard of again – again – again.'

Rilke, 'Orpheus. Eurydice. Hermes'

Orpheus desperate to get her back. But as Colm Tóibín, who chose the poem, writes: 'The dead will not come back, but the words will . . . filled with sad wisdom as the woman who was so loved will move into eternity, or nothing much, or perhaps nothing at all . . .'

Cavafy, 'Ithaka'

Not a dirge of dire loss and sorrow, but a zestful, thrilling command to the spirit of living fully, from the sensual 'may you stop at Phoenician trading stations' (twenty-first century traditional arts-and-crafts markets?) 'to buy fine things / . . . mother of pearl / . . . sensual perfumes'.

And on the serious side, 'may you visit many Egyptian cities / to gather stores of knowledge' (contemporary outer-space exploration centres!). While seeking fulfilment, 'keep Ithaka always in your mind / Arriving there is what you are destined for.' But what Ithaka gave you is 'the marvellous journey. / Without her you would not have set out. / She has nothing left to give you now.'

Tagore, 'Let My Country Awake'

In perhaps the most overtly political poem here, along with Shelley's 'The Masque of Anarchy', Tagore brings private ethics alongside civic responsibility as he sees that his country, India, must rouse itself: to where 'knowledge is free . . . the world has not been broken up into fragments by narrow domestic walls . . . the clear stream of reason has not lost its way into the dreary desert sand of dead habit.' The mind is led forward to the 'heaven of freedom'. However, he conceives that heaven to be reached by the path of religious faith called upon. 'Into that freedom, my Father, let my country awake.'

Auden, 'In Memory of W. B. Yeats'

'The day of his death was a dark cold day / . . . But for him it was his last afternoon as himself. . . . the words of a dead man. / When the brokers are roaring like beasts on the floor of the bourse . . . / And the poor have the sufferings to which they are fairly accustomed. / You were silly like us; your gift survived it all: the parish of rich women, physical decay . . .

'Mad Ireland hurt you into poetry.' Mad Africa, mad world, does this for the great ones' successors?

Brecht, 'The Book Burnings'

'When the Regime commanded that books with harmful knowledge / should be publicly burned and on all sides / oxen were forced to drag cartloads of books / to the bonfires, a banished / writer whose 'books had been passed over . . . wrote a letter to those in power / Burn me! . . . Haven't my books / Always reported the truth? . . . And here you are treating me like a liar / I command you: Burn me!'

I read this poem today in twenty-first-century South Africa, where the Protection of State Information bill is about to be adopted – here, another secrecy act about to become law moves Jack Mapanje, who chose the poem, to tears of ironic laughter.

Porter, 'An Exequy'

'When your slim shape from photographs / Stands at my door and gently asks / If I have any work to do / Or will I come to bed with you . . .' Ian McEwan, who chose this poem, writes 'now that Peter has gone and that deeply troubled marriage is a faded memory, this evocation of domestic intimacy, which is also a ghostly beckoning towards death, seems all the more poignant.' For me, this poem could bring a man, fearful of such loss in his own life, close to emotional breakdown.

Bishop, 'Crusoe in England'

Tactile imagery – so that on reading, this poem is with one's flesh, a personal living experience. Crusoe's island from the reversed loneliness of a different exile, in England: 'My island seemed to be / a sort of cloud-dump. All the hemisphere's / left-over clouds . . . their parched throats / were hot to touch . . . I often gave way to self-pity / "Do I deserve this? I suppose I must . . . Was there a moment when I actually chose this?"' Then his desperate loneliness: 'Just when I thought I couldn't stand it / another minute longer, Friday came . . . / Friday was nice and we were friends / If only he had been a woman! / I wanted to propagate my kind.' The power of the poet's imaginative creation, as personalities of familiar emotional legends are here brought face-to-face, alive with our present.

Everyone who reads this collection will be roused: disturbed by the pain, exalted in the zest for joy given by poets, all the way from 'Elegy' to 'eulogy to a hell of a dame' to 'An End or A Beginning'.

Nadine Gordimer (1923–2014) was a South African writer and political activist. The author of numerous novels, short stories and essay collections, she was awarded the 1991 Nobel Prize for Literature.

Acknowledgments

The editors wish to acknowledge the inspiration of the late Josephine Hart and her husband Maurice Saatchi, as well as William Sieghart and iF Poems in the UK, and Billy Collins in the USA, in their tireless efforts to bring poetry to a wider audience – just a few examples of trailblazers we very much hope to emulate with this anthology.

We profoundly thank Amnesty International for its enthusiastic partnership, especially Nicky Parker for her invaluable skills, alongside those of her colleagues Maggie Paterson and Lucy MacNamara in London and Carol Gregory and Suzanne Trimel in New York.

Margaret Jull Costa was kind enough to provide us with fresh translations of Spanish poetry. We are also grateful to A. S. Kline, Hyde Flippo and Terry Lajtha for their translations of German and French poems. Graham Henderson and Gabby Meadows of Poet in the City, London, were also encouraging supporters.

For help in locating or following up with contributors, or other such assistance, we are indebted to: Sven Becker, Cindy Blake, Carol Blue, Felicity Blunt, Mary Bly, Lucy Bright, Tina Brown, Ed Clarke, Rita Cruise O'Brien, Joe Dunthorne, Isabel Freer, Natalie Galustian, Heather Glen, Lars Knudsen, Damon Lane, Seb Loden, Jillian Longnecker, John Martin, Alex Moorehead, John David Morley, Kathy Robbins, Shira Rockowitz, Mary Jane Skalski, Joe Shrapnel, Anna Waterhouse, Jane Wellesley, and Catherine Williams. Many other friends, agents and their assistants have also gone to some trouble to help us along the way; we apologise for not naming them all here.

Alexander Hammond displayed considerable energy and persistence in hunting down copyright holders and negotiating on our behalves. For help in the home straight with this mammoth task, we thank Fred Courtright and Amanda Sumner. We are also grateful, as ever, to our representatives Gill Coleridge and Cara Jones of Rogers, Coleridge and White.

Dr Ad Vingerhoets, Professor of Clinical Psychology at Holland's Tilburg University, author of *Why Only Humans Weep*, kindly fact-checked Ben's preface on the mechanics of crying, which was also informed by Dr Tom Lutz's incisive study *Crying: A Natural and Cultural History of Tears*.

All Holdens in both our lives have lent valuable support and assistance, especially Salome, George, Ione, Amanda, Sam, Ursula, Rosemary, and Joe. Particular thanks to Salome for her generous help with an unusually complex set of proofs.

We are especially grateful to Ian Chapman and Suzanne Baboneau of Simon & Schuster UK for their faith in the project from the outset, and to their colleagues Helen Mockridge, Rik Ubhi and Sarah Birdsey. Similar thanks go to Jon Karp, Michael Szczerban and their colleagues at Simon & Schuster US. Many writers on both sides of the Atlantic are familiar with the rapier-sharp verbal acumen of our commissioning editor Richard Cohen; we are pleased to add our names to the list.

Above all, we wish to thank our contributors for so generously giving of their time and energy not merely in sharing a poem that they cannot read without a tear, but in taking the trouble to explain why. We are also, of course, very much in the debt of the poets themselves, and will always remain so.

Amnesty International

Poetry as an art form almost certainly predates literacy. Early poets must have performed their work, using the power of its tight structure, rhythms and cadences to stir their listeners, but also to lodge words in their memories. Poetry still touches hearts and minds, even in our digital world.

One of Amnesty's first prisoners of conscience was the Angolan poet and doctor Agostinho Neto. He suffered terrible brutality at the hands of the ruling Portuguese authorities before becoming the first President of Angola. Like Neto, all poets rely on the human right to freedom of expression, but throughout history they have been amongst the first targeted by repressive governments, presumably because of their power to stir emotions and liberate ideas.

Being jailed, however, isn't a great poetry deterrent. Many turn to it for comfort in the darkest of times. Guantánamo prisoners inscribed poems on polystyrene cups in the days before they were allowed paper. Malawian Jack Mapanje used his malaria tablets to write poems on the floor of his cell. Soviet prisoner poet Irena Ratuschinskaya scratched verses onto bars of soap with a pin or the burnt end of a matchstick, memorised them and then washed them off. Realising Irina was desperate for paper, her husband wrote her abusive letters that he knew would be delivered, concentrating his messages into a small square that left a large blank margin for her to write. Such was her desperation to express herself through poetry.

A particular characteristic of poetry is that its writers tend to pay minutely close attention to their subject matter. By using intimate details to express universal truths, they make us feel *'that could be me'*. As Melvyn Bragg says, 'all great poems are about each one of us'. The poet's insights are transmitted to the reader. It's a two-way creative process that liberates and enlightens both parties, and it lies at the crux of why our human right to freedom of expression is so important. Tom McCarthy puts it well: '. . . how people struggle to connect with art. And how the artist struggles to connect with his audience and remain true to . . . well, the truth. Regardless of the side you play for, citizen or artist, the need to reach out, to connect, to feel, and to affect is so satisfying and so elusive.'

This anthology might be accused of sexism because it deliberately excludes women contributors. Others may mock the very idea of men crying over poetry. But this is another reason why we at Amnesty are interested in it. It directly addresses the assumption bordering on cliché that women are more emotional – weaker – than men. Yet the contributions are all written by successful, influential men (some with very tough images) who admit to crying. Many share deeply personal insights and experiences, all provoked by poetry. Their emotional honesty is a healthy contrast to the behaviour that most societies expect of men. We know that bottling up emotions can lead to aggression. More than this, gender stereotyping is dangerous because it represses ability and ambition, it encourages discrimination and it upholds social inequalities that are a root cause of violence. We hope that this anthology will encourage boys, in particular, to know that crying (and poetry) isn't just for girls.

Writing poetry – or responding to it – happens because *people care*. And it's our capacity for caring that underpins our human rights.

Individuals who care have real power to make a difference. Amnesty International, now a global movement of some three million people, began because of one man's outrage and his courage to do something about it. It was 1961 when the lawyer Peter Benenson read about two Portuguese students imprisoned for toasting freedom, was inspired to take action and called on others to join him. This anthology is emblematic of the human struggle to make a difference, and we at Amnesty are profoundly grateful to all the contributors. Most of all, we thank Anthony and Ben Holden for their generosity in sharing this project with us.

Please see how you can make a difference by contacting us at Amnesty.

Kate Allen, Director
Amnesty International UK
The Human Rights Action Centre
17–25 New Inn Yard
London EC2A 3EA
www.amnesty.org.uk

Amnesty International USA
5 Penn Plaza,
New York,
NY 10001
www.amnestyusa.org

Index of Contributors and Poets

Italic page numbers refer to works of poetry.

Index of Titles of Poems

Index of First Lines

Credits, Copyrights, and Permissions

Note: The texts of those poems first written in languages other than English are included only at the specific request of the contributor or where the original text is directly referenced within the relevant introduction.

The editors gratefully acknowledge permission to reprint copyright material in this collection as follows below.

Francisco de Quevedo, 'Amor Constante más allá de la muerte' English translation, 'Love Constant Beyond Death' by Margaret Jull Costa, copyright © Margaret Jull Costa, 2014.

Ariel Dorfman's introduction to 'Amor Constante más allá de la muerte' copyright © Ariel Dorfman, 2014.

Fukuda Chiyo-ni, 'Hokku', English translation by Boris Akunin, copyright © Boris Akunin, 2014.

Johann Wolfgang von Goethe, translation of 'Wandrers Nachtlied II' copyright © Hyde Flippo, 2013.

Extract from *The Great War for Civilisation: The Conquest of the Middle East* by Robert Fisk, copyright © 2005, Robert Fisk. Reprinted by permission of HarperCollins Publishers Ltd.

Henrik Ibsen, excerpt from *Peer Gynt: A Dramatic Poem*, translated by Christopher Fry. Copyright © 1970 by Christopher Fry and Johan Fillinger. Reprinted by permission of Oxford University Press.

A. E. Housman, 'The Remorseful Day' ('How clear, how lovely bright'), 'Last Poems: XL', from *The Collected Poems of A. E. Housman*. Copyright 1939, 1940 by Holt, Rinehart and Winston, Inc. Copyright © 1967 by Robert E. Symons. Reprinted by permission of Henry Holt and Company, LLC.

Antonio Machado, 'Llamo a mi corazon, un claro dia/ The wind, one brilliant day, called', from *Times Alone: Selected Poems Of Antonio Machado*, translation copyright © 1983 by Robert Bly. Reprinted by permission of Wesleyan University Press.

Rainer Maria Rilke, 'Orpheus. Eurydice. Hermes.' translation copyright © 1982 by Stephen Mitchell, from *The Selected Poetry Of Rainer Maria Rilke*, translated by Stephen Mitchell. Used by permission of Random House, an imprint of the Random House Publishing Group, a division of Random House LLC. All rights reserved.

C. P. Cavafy, 'Ithaka' copyright © C. P. Cavafy. English translation copyright © Edmund Keeley and Philip Sherrard. Reproduced by permission of the authors c/o Rogers, Coleridge & White Ltd, 20 Powis Mews, London W11 1JN.

Extract from *Unacknowledged Legislation: Writers in the Public Sphere* by Christopher Hitchens, reprinted by permission of Carol Blue Hitchens. Copyright © Christopher Hitchens, 2000.

Siegfried Sassoon, 'Everyone Sang' copyright © Siegfried Sassoon, reprinted by permission of the Estate of George Sassoon.

Gabriela Mistral, 'God Wills It', from *The Selected Poems of Gabriela Mistral*, translated by Ursula K. Le Guin. Copyright © University of New Mexico Press, 2003.

Robert Graves, 'The Cool Web', from *Poems 1914–1926* (London: William Heinemann, 1927). Later in *Complete Poems in One Volume,* edited by

Beryl Grave and Dustan Ward (Manchester: Carcanet, 2000), reprinted by permission of Carcanet Press Ltd and United Agents on behalf of the Trustees of the Robert Graves Copyright Trust.

Introduction to 'The Broken Tower' copyright © Harold Bloom. Reprinted by permission of Harold Bloom and Yale University Press.

W. H. Auden, 'A Summer Night' copyright © 1937 by Random House, Inc. and renewed 1965 by W. H. Auden, used by permission of Random House, Inc, and Curtis Brown, Ltd.

'In Memory of W. B. Yeats' copyright © 1940 and renewed 1968 by W. H. Auden, used by permission of Random House, Inc, and Curtis Brown, Ltd.

'Lullaby' copyright © 1940 and renewed 1968 by W. H. Auden, used by permission of Random House, Inc, and Curtis Brown, Ltd.

Extract from 'Their Lovely Betters' and 'Funeral Blues/Stop All The Clocks' copyright © by W. H. Auden. Used by permission of Random House, Inc, and Curtis Brown, Ltd.

'If I Could Tell You' copyright © 1945 by W. H. Auden and renewed 1973 by the Estate of W. H. Auden, used by permission of Random House, Inc, and Curtis Brown, Ltd.

Alexander McCall Smith's introduction to 'If I Could Tell You' copyright © Alexander McCall Smith, 2014.

Keith Douglas, 'Canoe', from *The Collected Poems*, © 1998, the Estate of Keith Douglas. Reprinted by permission of Faber & Faber Ltd and Faber and Faber, Inc., an affiliate of Farrar, Straus, Giroux, LLC.

Theodore Roethke, 'My Papa's Waltz', from *Collected Poems*. Copyright © Theodore Roethke. Reproduced by permission of Faber & Faber, Ltd, and Random House, Inc.

Bertolt Brecht, 'The Book Burnings', originally published in Germans as 'Die Bucherverbrennung'. Copyright © 2014 by Thomas Mark Kuhn and David J Constantine. Copyright 1939 © by Bertolt-Brecht-Erben/ Suhrkamp Verlag.

Paul Éluard, 'Liberté' translation copyright © A. S. Kline, 2014. Reprinted with the permission of the translator and Les Editions de Minuit S.A.

Excerpts from *The Cantos Of Ezra Pound* copyright © 1948 by Ezra Pound. Reprinted by permission of New Directions Publishing Corp and Faber & Faber, Ltd

Philip Larkin, 'I see a girl dragged by the wrists', 'Unfinished Poem' and 'Aubade', from *The Complete Poems Of Philip Larkin*, edited by Archie Burnett. Copyright © 2012 by the Estate of Philip Larkin. Reprinted by permission of Faber & Faber Ltd and Farrar, Straus, Giroux, LLC.

Gwendolyn Brooks, 'The Mother' copyright © Gwendolyn Brooks. Reprinted by consent of Brooks Permissions.

Extract from 'The Fury of Aerial Bombardment', from *Collected Poems 1930–1986*. Copyright © 1960, 1976, 1987 by Richard Eberhart. By permission of Oxford University Press USA, and the Richard Eberhart Estate.

Randall Jarrell, 'The Death of the Ball Turret Gunner', from *The Complete Poems*. Copyright © 1969, renewed 1997 by Mary von S. Jarrell. Reprinted by permission of Faber & Faber Ltd and Farrar, Straus, Giroux, LLC.

Berthold Brecht, 'War Has Been Brought Into Disrepute', originally published in German in 1964 as 'Der Krieg Ist Geschandet Worden'. Copyright © 2014 by Thomas Mark Kuhn and David J. Constantine. Copyright © 1964 by Bertolt-Brecht-Erben/Suhrkamp Verlag, from *Collected Poems Of Bertolt Brecht* by Bertolt Brecht, translated by Thomas Mark Kuhn and David J. Constantine. Used by permission of Liveright Publishing Corporation.

Jacques Prevért, 'Le Message' translation © Terry Lajtha, 2014. French © Éditions Gallimard, Paris, 1976. Reprinted by permission of Éditions Gallimard, Paris, and Terry Lajtha.

Elizabeth Bishop, 'Over 2,000 Illustrations and a Complete Concordance' and 'Crusoe in England', from *The Complete Poems 1927–1979*. Copyright © 1979, 1983 by Alice Helen Methfessel. Reprinted by permission of Farrar, Straus and Giroux, LLC.

John Ashbery's introduction to 'Over 2,000 Illustrations and a Complete Concordance' copyright © 2014, John Ashbery.

Stanley Kunitz, 'End of Summer', from *The Collected Poems*. Copyright © 1953 by Stanley Kunitz. Reprinted by permission of W. W. Norton & Company, Inc.

Edwin Muir, 'The Horses' © 1965 Edwin Muir, from *Collected Poems*. Reprinted by permission of the Estate of Edwin Muir and Faber and Faber Ltd.

W. H. Auden, 'Friday's Child' copyright © 1958 by W. H. Auden. Used by permission of Random House, Inc, and Curtis Brown, Ltd.

Tony Harrison, 'Long Distance I and II', from *Selected Poems*. Copyright © Tony Harrison. Reproduced by permission of the author, c/o Gordon Dickerson.

Les Murray, 'The Widower in the Country', from *Collected Poems* (*Rabbiter's Bounty* in the US), copyright © Les Murray, 1992. Reproduced by permission of Carcanet Press Ltd, and Farrar, Straus, Giroux, LLC.

Pablo Neruda, 'La Injusticia' translation copyright © Valeria Baker. Spanish © Fundación Pablo Neruda, 2014. Reprinted with the permission of the Carmen Balcells Agencia Literaria SA.

Abiosch Nicol, 'The Meaning of Africa'. Copyright © Abioseh Nicol. Reprinted by permission of Harold Ober Associates, Incorporated.

Christopher Okigbo, 'Elegy for Alto', from *Labyrinths with Path of Thunder*, copyright © Christopher Okigbo, 1971. Reprinted by permission of Pearson Education Ltd.

Seamus Heaney, 'Requiem For The Croppies' and 'A Call', from *Opened Ground: Selected Poems 1966–1996*. Copyright © 1998 by Seamus Heaney. Reprinted by permission of Faber & Faber Ltd and Farrar, Straus and Giroux, LLC.

Christopher Logue, 'Gone Ladies' copyright © the Estate of Christopher Logue. Reproduced by kind permission of the Estate of Christopher Logue.

John Berryman, 'Dream Song 90: Op. posth. no. 13', or 'On the Death of Randall Jarrell', from *Collected Poems: 1937–1971*. Copyright © 1989 by Kate Donahue Berryman. Reprinted by permission of Faber & Faber Ltd and Farrar, Straus, Giroux, LLC. Introduction to 'Dream Song 90' copyright © A. Alvarez, 1999. Reproduced by kind permission of the author.

Hayden Carruth, 'Essay', from *Brothers, I Loved You All: Poems 1969–1977*, ©1978, Hayden Carruth. Reprinted by permission of the Sheep Meadow Press.

Peter Porter, 'An Exequy', from *Collected Poems*, copyright © the Estate of Peter Porter. Reproduced by permission of the Estate c/o Rogers, Coleridge & White Ltd.

John N. Morris, 'For Julia, in the Deep Water' from *The Glass Houses*. Reprinted by kind permission of the Estate of John N. Morris.

W. S. Graham: 'Dear Bryan Wynter', from *New Collected Poems* (Faber and Faber, 2004), © the Estate of W. S. Graham, reprinted by permission of Rosalind Mudaliar, Administrator for the Estate of W. S. Graham.

Wendell Berry, 'A Meeting', from *New Collected Poems*, copyright © 2012 by Wendell Berry. Used by permission of Counterpoint.

Charles Bukowski, 'eulogy to a hell of a dame' from *The Pleasures Of The Damned*. Copyright © 2007, Linda Lee Bukowski. Reprinted by permission of HarperCollins Publishers.

Derek Walcott, 'Sonnet XLIII' and 'Love After Love', from *Midsummer*, from *Collected Poems 1948–1984*. Copyright © 1986 by Derek Walcott. Reprinted by permission of Faber & Faber Ltd and Farrar, Straus and Giroux, LLC.

Mary Oliver, 'In Blackwater Woods', from *American Primitive*. Copyright © 1978, 1979, 1980, 1981, 1982, 1983 by Mary Oliver. By permission of Little, Brown and Company. All rights reserved.

John Berger, extract from and *our faces, my heart, brief as photos*. Copyright © 1984 by John Berger. Used by permission of the Wylie Agency and Pantheon Books, an imprint of the Knopf Doubleday Publishing Group, a division of Random House LLC. All rights reserved.

Douglas Dunn, 'Sandra's Mobile', from *Elegies*. Reproduced by permission of Faber & Faber Ltd and United Agents on behalf of Douglas Dunn.

Mauricio Rosencof, 'Brindis Con El Viejo', translated by Margaret Jull Costa. Translation copyright © 2014, Margaret Jull Costa. Extract of the book *Memorias del calabozo*, Ediciones de la Banda Oriental, Montevideo 1987–88. © Mauricio Rosencof 1987. By arrangement with Literarische Agentur Mertin Inh. Nicole Witt e. K., Frankfurt am Main, Germany.

Bei Dao, 'An End or A Beginning', translated by Bonnie S. McDougall, from *The August Sleepwalker*, copyright ©1988 by Bei Dao. Translation copyright © 1988, 1990 by Bonnie S. McDougall. Reprinted by permission of New Directions Publishing Corp and Anvil Press Poetry Ltd.

Adrienne Rich, Part Ten of 'Eastern War Time', from *An Atlas Of The Difficult World: Poems 1988–1991*. Copyright © 1991 by Adrienne Rich. Used by permission of W. W. Norton & Company, Inc.

James Wright, 'A Blessing', from *Collected Poems*. Copyright © 1971, James Wright. Reprinted by permission of Wesleyan University Press.

Harold Pinter, 'It Is Here', from *Various Voices*. Copyright © 1998 by Harold Pinter. Used by permission of Faber and Faber Ltd and Grove/Atlantic, Inc. Any third party use of this material, outside of this publication, is prohibited.

James Fenton, 'For Andrew Wood', from *Out of Danger*, copyright © James Fenton, 1994. Reprinted by permission of United Agents on behalf of the author.

John Updike, 'Not Cancelled Yet', from *Higher Gossip: Essays and Criticism*, edited by Christopher Carduff. Copyright © 2011 by the Estate of John H. Updike. Reprinted by permission of Penguin Books Ltd and Alfred A. Knopf, an imprint of the Knopf Doubleday Publishing Group, a division of Random House LLC. All rights reserved.

Brian Patten, 'Armada' copyright © Brian Patten, 1996. Reproduced by permission of the author c/o Rogers, Coleridge & White Ltd, 20 Powis Mews, London NW1 0JG.

William Matthews, 'A Poetry Reading at West Point' rom *After All: Last*

Poems. Copyright ©1998 by the Estate of William Matthews. Reprinted by permission of the Houghton Mifflin Company. All rights reserved.

Victoria Redel, 'Bedecked', from *Swoon* (University of Chicago Press). Copyright © Victoria Redel, 2003. Reprinted by kind permission of the author.

Billy Collins, 'The Lanyard', from *The Trouble With Poetry: And Other Poems*. Copyright © 2005, Billy Collins. Used by permission of Random House, Inc.

Emily Zinnemann, 'Regarding the home of one's childhood, one could:' copyright © Emily Zinnemann. Reprinted by kind permission of the author.

Craig Raine, 'For Ruthie Rogers in Venice' copyright © Craig Raine, 2010. Reprinted by kind permission of the author.

Robin Robertson, 'Keys to the Doors', from *Hill of Doors*. Copyright © Robin Robertson, 2012. Reproduced by permission of the author c/o Rogers, Coleridge & White Ltd, 20 Powis Mews, London NW1 0JG.

Mohsin Hamid's introduction to 'Keys to the Door' Copyright © Mohsin Hamid, 2014.

Afterword by Nadine Gordimer: Copyright © Nadine Gordimer, 2014.

Coming in Spring 2016, the perfect companion volume

POEMS THAT MAKE GROWN WOMEN CRY

Another remarkable anthology of poetry, this time
chosen by 100 eminent women from all walks of life

Edited by Anthony and Ben Holden
And once again in partnership with Amnesty International